[H.A.S.C. No. 113–78]

UNITED STATES SECURITY POLICY AND DEFENSE POSTURE IN THE MIDDLE EAST

COMMITTEE ON ARMED SERVICES
HOUSE OF REPRESENTATIVES

ONE HUNDRED THIRTEENTH CONGRESS

SECOND SESSION

HEARING HELD
FEBRUARY 11, 2014

U.S. GOVERNMENT PRINTING OFFICE

86–968   WASHINGTON : 2014

COMMITTEE ON ARMED SERVICES

ONE HUNDRED THIRTEENTH CONGRESS

HOWARD P. "BUCK" McKEON, California, *Chairman*

MAC THORNBERRY, Texas
WALTER B. JONES, North Carolina
J. RANDY FORBES, Virginia
JEFF MILLER, Florida
JOE WILSON, South Carolina
FRANK A. LoBIONDO, New Jersey
ROB BISHOP, Utah
MICHAEL R. TURNER, Ohio
JOHN KLINE, Minnesota
MIKE ROGERS, Alabama
TRENT FRANKS, Arizona
BILL SHUSTER, Pennsylvania
K. MICHAEL CONAWAY, Texas
DOUG LAMBORN, Colorado
ROBERT J. WITTMAN, Virginia
DUNCAN HUNTER, California
JOHN FLEMING, Louisiana
MIKE COFFMAN, Colorado
E. SCOTT RIGELL, Virginia
CHRISTOPHER P. GIBSON, New York
VICKY HARTZLER, Missouri
JOSEPH J. HECK, Nevada
JON RUNYAN, New Jersey
AUSTIN SCOTT, Georgia
STEVEN M. PALAZZO, Mississippi
MO BROOKS, Alabama
RICHARD B. NUGENT, Florida
KRISTI L. NOEM, South Dakota
PAUL COOK, California
JIM BRIDENSTINE, Oklahoma
BRAD R. WENSTRUP, Ohio
JACKIE WALORSKI, Indiana
BRADLEY BYRNE, Alabama

ADAM SMITH, Washington
LORETTA SANCHEZ, California
MIKE McINTYRE, North Carolina
ROBERT A. BRADY, Pennsylvania
ROBERT E. ANDREWS, New Jersey
SUSAN A. DAVIS, California
JAMES R. LANGEVIN, Rhode Island
RICK LARSEN, Washington
JIM COOPER, Tennessee
MADELEINE Z. BORDALLO, Guam
JOE COURTNEY, Connecticut
DAVID LOEBSACK, Iowa
NIKI TSONGAS, Massachusetts
JOHN GARAMENDI, California
HENRY C. "HANK" JOHNSON, JR., Georgia
COLLEEN W. HANABUSA, Hawaii
JACKIE SPEIER, California
RON BARBER, Arizona
ANDRE CARSON, Indiana
CAROL SHEA-PORTER, New Hampshire
DANIEL B. MAFFEI, New York
DEREK KILMER, Washington
JOAQUIN CASTRO, Texas
TAMMY DUCKWORTH, Illinois
SCOTT H. PETERS, California
WILLIAM L. ENYART, Illinois
PETE P. GALLEGO, Texas
MARC A. VEASEY, Texas

ROBERT L. SIMMONS II, *Staff Director*
ALEXANDER GALLO, *Professional Staff Member*
MICHAEL CASEY, *Professional Staff Member*
AARON FALK, *Clerk*

CONTENTS

CHRONOLOGICAL LIST OF HEARINGS

2014

TUESDAY, FEBRUARY 11, 2014

UNITED STATES SECURITY POLICY AND DEFENSE POSTURE IN THE MIDDLE EAST

STATEMENTS PRESENTED BY MEMBERS OF CONGRESS

WITNESSES

APPENDIX

UNITED STATES SECURITY POLICY AND DEFENSE POSTURE IN THE MIDDLE EAST

HOUSE OF REPRESENTATIVES,
COMMITTEE ON ARMED SERVICES,
Washington, DC, Tuesday, February 11, 2014.

The committee met, pursuant to call, at 10:00 a.m., in room 2118, Rayburn House Office Building, Hon. Howard P. "Buck" McKeon (chairman of the committee) presiding.

OPENING STATEMENT OF HON. HOWARD P. "BUCK" MCKEON, A REPRESENTATIVE FROM CALIFORNIA, CHAIRMAN, COMMITTEE ON ARMED SERVICES

The CHAIRMAN. The committee will come to order. Good morning, ladies and gentlemen. We appreciate all of you being here today. The committee meets to receive testimony on United States security policy and defense posture in the Middle East.

And I just want to point out before we begin that there will be no disruptions at the hearing. We appreciate you all cooperating for that to make sure that everything goes well.

Our witnesses today include Ambassador Anne Patterson; Ms. Elissa—Elissa, I have got a granddaughter, Elissa—Slotkin; and Vice Admiral Frank Pandolfe.

Thank you all for joining us here today.

The committee has conducted several classified briefings and open hearings with outside experts on this topic area. However, today is an opportunity to build upon that knowledge in an open forum with senior policy and military leaders in our government. The Middle East is in the midst of a particularly tumultuous period, from the Arab Awakening to the evolution of Al Qaeda, to the deadly conflict in Syria, to Iran's continued pursuit of nuclear weapons. We are witnessing a level of volatility in the Middle East that poses a serious threat to U.S. security and to our interests in the region.

While our allies and partners seek strong U.S. leadership and engagement in the region, they instead see signs of disengagement. Our withdrawals from Iraq and Afghanistan, the administration's rebalance to other regions and its dealmaking with Iran help shape this view. There is widespread uncertainty about U.S. commitment in the Middle East.

As noted by former U.N. [United Nations] Ambassador to Iraq James Jeffrey in a recent op-ed, and I quote, "As often happens in this region, the administration is sounding an uncertain tone. The result has been an extraordinary collapse of U.S. credibility in the region, despite many commendable administration steps," end quote. These comments illustrate a lack of certainty about U.S. policy in the region.

Equally important is our military posture in the region, how we combat evolving threats, deter Iran, degrade Al Qaeda, and assure our allies and partners. We also must ensure our military posture and its associated capabilities are not traded for interim deals with regimes that have a history of noncompliance.

We look forward to your testimony on the administration's policy and posture in the Middle East and how they comprehensively support U.S. national security interests.

Now I will turn to Ranking Member Smith for his statement.

[The prepared statement of Mr. McKeon can be found in the Appendix on page 41.]

STATEMENT OF HON. ADAM SMITH, A REPRESENTATIVE FROM WASHINGTON, RANKING MEMBER, COMMITTEE ON ARMED SERVICES

Mr. SMITH. Thank you, Mr. Chairman.

Thanks to our exceptionally well qualified group of witnesses. Look forward to your testimony and discussion on this important region.

It is a complex and difficult region, perhaps as complex as it has ever been for us with the Arab Awakening; our, you know, presence in Iraq and then withdrawal from Iraq and now the difficulties that are there; Syrian civil war; transition governments in Egypt, Tunisia, and a whole lot of other places; and an ongoing effort, once again, to try to reach and resolve the Israeli-Palestinian crisis. I cannot imagine a more difficult set of challenges.

And I think our commitment to the region is clear. I will disagree with the chairman on that. I mean, our efforts to negotiate with Iran are an effort to resolve what is an incredibly difficult tension. We do not want Iran to have a nuclear weapon. And if we are going to prevent them from doing that, we need to actively engage, which I believe that we are.

I also, you know, very much support Secretary Kerry's efforts to, once again, try to resolve the Israeli-Palestinian crisis, which is a major source of tension in the region and significant uncertainty for Israeli allies.

I think we are committed and engaged in the region. The problem is it is a very difficult region. And the thing I am most interested in is how do we work in that region, understanding that we cannot control it? And I think that is the problem with some of the analysis out there as if the U.S. simply woke up one day and decided to be more engaged, everyone would listen to us and, you know, solve all of their problems. You know, one of our problems and challenges in the region is understandably that region wants to be autonomous. They do not want to think that the U.S. is the one that is going to show up and solve their problems.

And also to be perfectly honest, we have some credibility issues in that region. You know, people, you know, you saw in Egypt, you know, both sides were claiming that the reason that Egyptians should support them is because the U.S. was supporting the other side. You know, that lack of credibility undermines our ability to simply show up, have a presence, and fix problems. It creates a very complex diplomatic set of circumstances.

So I am very interested to hear from our witnesses how we manage that, how we do stay involved, because I think it is critical that we do, but stay involved in a way that is positive and helpful and understanding the limitations on our ability to simply show up and solve these problems in a region that ultimately is going to have to solve its own problems. How do we balance those challenges?

You know, I think the administration is having a clear message, and it is trying to do that, but it is a difficult, complicated region. So I look forward to your testimony explaining how we can navigate those very, very challenging set of circumstances that exist in the Middle East. And I thank you for being here, and I look forward to your testimony and the questions that follow.

[The prepared statement of Mr. Smith can be found in the Appendix on page 42.]

The CHAIRMAN. Thank you.

Ambassador Patterson.

STATEMENT OF AMBASSADOR ANNE W. PATTERSON, ASSISTANT SECRETARY OF STATE FOR NEAR EASTERN AFFAIRS, U.S. DEPARTMENT OF STATE

Ambassador PATTERSON. Thank you, Mr. Chairman, Ranking Member——

The CHAIRMAN. Ambassador, you are going to have to just pretend like you are——

Ambassador PATTERSON. Thank you.

The CHAIRMAN [continuing]. A rock star and swallow that microphone.

Ambassador PATTERSON. Thank you.

The CHAIRMAN. It really only picks it up if you are right——

Ambassador PATTERSON. Close to it.

Thank you, Mr. Chairman, Ranking Member Smith, members of the committee. I am honored to appear before you today with my colleagues from the Defense Department. Together with the Intelligence Community, we work to protect our country from terrorist attacks and to promote American national security objectives.

The Middle East today is undergoing historic changes. Across the region, we are seeing unprecedented political ferment and in some cases upheaval as people demand change. There are deep demographic and economic forces that add urgency to this situation, but it is clear that the forces of change are knocking down some of the longstanding pillars that have supported regional stability. Regrettably, there are no easy solutions.

The rapid pace of events in the region also threatens to open long dormant divisions within societies, among class, sect, religion, and ethnicity. These developments feed revolutionary sentiment and set the conditions for extremism that is rejected by the vast majority of people across the region and poses a threat to the United States.

The United States is and will remain firmly engaged in the Middle East. Our relationships in the region make the United States an essential player in the search for diplomatic solutions. The region's people want effective governments that respect universal rights, presenting us with opportunities to show the way. Our position in the global economy can help both ourselves and the region through broader trade and investment. Secretary of State Kerry has undertaken extraordinary efforts to address the region's pressing and interrelated challenges and leading efforts to prevent Iran from obtaining a nuclear weapon, to end the civil war in Syria, and to help reach a final status agreement between the Israelis and Palestinians.

Mr. Chairman, I know this committee shares our deep concern about Iran's nuclear program. The United States is firmly committed to preventing Iran from acquiring a nuclear weapon. Talks on a comprehensive solution will begin in Vienna next week. Meanwhile, we can continue to enforce vigorously the existing sanctions put in place by the United States and many in the international community.

We are also well aware that Iran continues to promote regional instability through both Iranian and proxy fighters. Iran's support for Hezbollah has done much to destabilize Lebanon, promote tensions along Israel's northern border, and help keep the Assad regime in power. Iran is also working to undermine Yemen's peaceful transition and Bahrain's stability. Our negotiations with Iran on the nuclear issue will not stop us from taking decisive steps with our partners in the Gulf, in Europe, and elsewhere, to end these and other dangerous activities.

In Iraq, Mr. Chairman, Iraq has been experiencing escalating levels of violence. The two-way flow of extremists between Iraq and Syria has allowed high-profile attacks in Iraq, mostly led by fighters from the Islamic State of Iraq and the Levant, ISIL, formerly known as Al Qaeda in Iraq. Taking advantage of Iraq's fragility and government weakness, ISIL began shifting resources from Syria to Iraq last year, consistent with its broader ambitions. By last summer, they were launching between 30 and 40 suicide bombings monthly. In January, ISIL attacked and occupied Ramadi and Fallujah. Working with local leaders, the government has largely freed Ramadi of ISIL and its plans to clear Fallujah—and it plans to clear Fallujah using mostly tribal forces.

I would like to thank the Congress for supporting the much needed military equipment we have been able to provide to Iraq. The government needs a professional and well-equipped army to engage extremist groups before they enter the cities.

The growing violence has had a devastating effect on Iraq's people. To repair the damage, Iraq's political leaders must work together urgently across religious and ethnic divides on essential political reforms in advance of April 30th national elections.

Mr. Chairman, 3 years ago in Syria, a series of peaceful protests against the Assad regime were met with violence and repression. The ensuing civil war has caused enormous destruction and terrible hardships for the Syrian people. It has also had serious consequences for Syria's neighbors, Turkey, Lebanon, and Jordan, as well as Iraq.

The United States has responded to this crisis by providing more than $1.7 billion in a humanitarian assistance, the largest of any nation, for people affected by the conflict inside Syria and across the region. The Assad regime has responded with obstruction and delay, preventing aid from reaching more than 250,000 civilians.

Although there has been modest progress in Homs, civilians remain trapped in the cities of East Ghouta and Mouadamiya. The conflict has become a magnet for extremists from around the world trying to hijack the Syrians' aspirations. We assess there are nearly 26,000 extremist fighters in Syria, including more than 7,000 foreign fighters from up to 50 countries. Many are affiliated with designated terrorist groups, such as the Al-Nusra Front and ISIL, openly competing with the moderate Syrian opposition and the regime.

The United States has worked to build an international consensus for ending this conflict. Although the Geneva II process has begun, supported by over 40 nations and international organizations, it initiates a process that can only end with the Assad regime's departure. Our team is in Geneva today seeking progress on discussions toward a transition process and steps to ensure humanitarian access to the civilians trapped by the conflict.

We are working closely with international partners to support the Organization for the Prohibition of Chemical Weapons [OPCW] to meet the ambitious June 30th target date for the elimination of Syria's chemical weapons program. The OPCW has destroyed all of Syria's chemical weapons production and mixing equipment, and the U.S. and others are working with them to destroy remaining chemical weapons and precursors. We are concerned about the Syrian government's slow pace and are working with the international community to press them to fulfill their international obligations.

Mr. Chairman, the United States will remain engaged in resolving some of the region's major international political crises. We will use our influence to press for political reforms and democratic governments that respects universal rights, enabling societies to change and adapt, and we will press for economic reforms and seek to expand trade and investment to provide jobs, opportunities and hope that will benefit people in the region and the United States. Progress in these three areas can help turn the extraordinary creativity and energy of people in this region toward the building of a better future. It will take years of work, but our national security depends upon it. Thank you.

[The prepared statement of Ambassador Patterson can be found in the Appendix on page 44.]

The CHAIRMAN. Thank you.

Ms. Slotkin.

STATEMENT OF ELISSA SLOTKIN, PRINCIPAL DEPUTY ASSISTANT SECRETARY OF DEFENSE FOR INTERNATIONAL SECURITY AFFAIRS, U.S. DEPARTMENT OF DEFENSE

Ms. SLOTKIN. Thank you very much. Can you hear me? Does this work? Yeah.

The CHAIRMAN. Right into it.

Ms. SLOTKIN. Right into it. Okay.

Chairman McKeon, Ranking Member Smith and other distinguished members of the committee, I appreciate the opportunity to speak to you on both our multilateral and bilateral defense relationships in the Middle East and how these partnerships fit into our broader regional policy.

In broad terms, our strategy involves cooperating with regional partners and the international community in order to help foster a Middle East that is stable, peaceful, and prosperous and that, over time, succeeds in fulfilling the aspirations of its own people. The people in the region want a greater say in national affairs. They want broadening of human opportunity, and they want recognition of the rights and dignity of every individual.

The continuing ripples of the Arab Spring and the political transitions taking place in the Middle East offer the United States both opportunities and challenges as we work to address our core interests. Those interests are combating Al Qaeda and affiliated movements; confronting external aggression directed at our allies and partners; ensuring the free flow of energy to the rest of the world; and preventing the development, proliferation, and use of weapons of mass destruction.

Given the intersection of these four core interests, the greater Middle East remains a region of vital strategic importance to the United States. This is a point the administration has made repeatedly, including in the 2012 Defense Strategic Guidance, which affirms that, quote, "The United States will continue to place a premium on U.S. and allied military presence in and support of partner nations in and around the region," end quote.

At the core of this commitment are four critical tools that the Defense Department uses to achieve U.S. goals in the region: our force posture, our bilateral relationships, our growing multilateral relationships, and our military exercises across the region. I will briefly talk about each of these in turn.

First, our force posture: The most tangible sign of U.S. commitment that we can make to the security of the region is the physical presence of the men and women in uniform as well as the presence of advanced military equipment. Anyone, friend or foe, who looks at our presence in the Middle East will come to only one conclusion: our commitment to the Middle East is in no way eroding. We have ground, air, and naval presence of more than 35,000 U.S. forces in and around the immediate vicinity of the Gulf. We routinely maintain a naval presence of more than 40 ships, including a carrier strike group, and conduct a range of freedom of navigation operations. These operations have included approximately 50 transits of the Strait of Hormuz over the past 6 months. Taken together, the U.S. has the ability to project power in the region, deter our adversaries, and reassure our allies and partners.

Another critical tool, and one I cannot overstate, are bilateral relationships in the region. The Middle East is home to some of the most important bilateral security relationships we have anywhere in the world, and that starts, of course, with Israel. The U.S.-Israeli defense relationship remains stronger than ever. In addition to the State-led and DOD-executed [Department of Defense] Foreign Military Finance Program, DOD contributes to Israeli security by maintaining Israel's qualitative military edge and authorizing the sale of advanced technology to Israel. The U.S. is providing $3.1 billion in foreign military financing to Israel this year as part of a 10-year, $30 billion commitment to Israel. We are in near daily contact with our Israeli counterparts.

Another bilateral security relationship that is important to achieving U.S. goals in the region is our relationship with Egypt. The U.S.-Egypt relationship is one of our most significant and enduring defense relationships in the region. For more than 30 years, it has served to further our countries' joint security interests. Our bilateral partnership facilitates cooperation on counterterrorism, eases U.S. military access and critical overflight privileges, helps improve the security of Israel, and contributes to the security of our embassy and consulate. As we recalibrate the relationship in the wake of the Arab Spring, it by no means diminishes the importance that Egypt plays in the region.

Another important bilateral relationship that we continue to work on is with the government of Iraq. Since 2011, we have normalized our security cooperation with Iraq by forming the Office of Security Cooperation under the U.S. embassy and reducing its size from more than 700 uniformed military personnel to 108 personnel today.

We have been tracking the uptick in violence and the situation in Anbar, obviously, very closely. We, along with our State Department colleagues and others in the U.S. Government, have been urging the government of Iraq that the only long-term way to defeat the Islamic State of Iraq and the Levant, ISIL, is through robust cooperation with Sunni leaders, and we continue to encourage Prime Minister Maliki to address Sunni grievances. Iraq will only be secure when all Iraqis are included in the political, economic, and social life of the country.

Our bilateral relationships are critical, but our policy in the Middle East also depends on our growing multilateral ties. Our recent multilateral initiative was the President's determination to make the Gulf Cooperation Council, GCC, eligible to be furnished with U.S. defense articles and services as a single entity, a designation similar to NATO [North Atlantic Treaty Organization] or the African Union. This designation will help us work with our Gulf Cooperation Council member states to enhance critical capabilities, including items for ballistic missile defense, maritime security, and counterterrorism.

Of course, multilateral relationships are especially important in contexts where our national security depends on very broad diplomatic support. The United States continues to support the U.N.-Arab League Joint Special Representative Brahimi and the opposition in their efforts to find a negotiated political solution to the Syrian crisis and the creation of a transitional governing body within the framework of the Geneva communique.

We will also continue to closely watch the multilateral effort to ensure the destruction of Syria's chemical weapons arsenal. The Department of Defense has dispatched the naval vessel, *Cape Ray,* to receive Syrian chemicals and ultimately dispose of them ahead of the June deadline.

Another difficult regional situation that we have sought to address through multilateral engagement is the often destabilizing behavior of the government of Iran. Let me once again reiterate what this administration has said repeatedly: We will not allow Iran to acquire a nuclear weapon. Our strategy of pressure and engagement, a strategy made possible by strong multilateral sanctions, has created a window for diplomacy, and the Joint Plan of Action was an important first step. We are now focused on testing the prospects for our comprehensive nuclear deal, based on verifiable actions that convince us and the international community that Iran is not trying to obtain a nuclear bomb. The Department fully supports these diplomatic efforts while continuing to focus intently on ensuring that the President has all options available should negotiations falter or Iran not abide by its commitments.

Finally, the Department's military exercises help us advance security relationships in the Middle East, both bilateral and multilateral. I will allow my colleague, Vice Admiral Pandolfe, to provide more detail, but let me assure you, we are exercising with our partners in the air, on the ground, and at sea, improving experience in interoperability and working together on common security challenges.

Thank you, members of the committee, for this opportunity to discuss the primary tools we are using to advance our security priorities in the region. I look forward to your questions.

[The prepared statement of Ms. Slotkin can be found in the Appendix on page 57.]

The CHAIRMAN. Thank you.

Admiral.

STATEMENT OF VADM FRANK C. PANDOLFE, USN, DIRECTOR FOR STRATEGIC PLANS AND POLICY (J–5), JOINT STAFF, U.S. DEPARTMENT OF DEFENSE

Admiral PANDOLFE. Good morning, Chairman McKeon, Ranking Member Smith, and distinguished committee members. Thank you for this opportunity to update you regarding how our military forces are supporting U.S. policy objectives in the Middle East. Our vital interests in that unsettled part of the world are significant, and we are committed to working with the states of the region to strengthen security, enhance deterrence, and prevent war.

The U.S. seeks to increase regional stability, decrease violent extremism, and counter the proliferation and the use of weapons of mass destruction against our Nation, our allies, and our partners. We cannot do these things alone. Rather, to accomplish these goals, we work together every day with other agencies of our government, with forward station State Department professionals, and with partner countries in the region.

All of these missions require us to maintain significant combat power forward and to continually interact with our partners by way of operations, training, and investing in military-to-military relationships. Let me share a few examples.

Regarding operations, our forces in the Middle East operate continuously on the land, in the air, and on the sea, routinely conducting freedom of navigation operations, forward deployments, and port visits. They enhance stability and safeguard access to the global commons. U.S. military forces in the area are significant, with thousands of personnel deployed throughout the region, especially in and around the Arabian Gulf and in Afghanistan. Included in these numbers are U.S. soldiers and marines with armor, artillery, and attack helicopters; highly trained special operations forces; our most advanced aircraft; advanced surveillance assets; a wide array of missile defense capabilities, including ballistic missile defense ships and Patriot batteries; and a large naval presence, including a carrier strike group, mine-sweeping capabilities, and an afloat forward staging base.

Additionally, as mentioned, we conduct numerous exercises to increase the proficiency and the interoperability of our partners across all mission areas, including war fighting, counterterrorism, maritime security, and peacekeeping. U.S. CENTCOM's [Central Command] extensive exercise program includes, on average, 35 significant exercises each quarter. In 2013, our training efforts included Exercise Eagle Resolve, which was hosted by Qatar and included forces from 12 nations. Exercise Eager Lion in Jordan involved 8,000 personnel from 19 nations, and the International Mine Countermeasures Exercise in Bahrain included 40 nations and 35 ships. These are just a few of the hundreds of engagements conducted by all services with foreign partners each year.

In conjunction with the Department of State, our military also maintains an aggressive schedule of leader interactions to strengthen relationships. These help us better understand regional perspectives on common security issues while fostering cooperation. For example, Chairman Dempsey participated in the Middle East Chiefs of Defense Conference in Jordan last August. Also CENTCOM Commander, General Austin, and his service component commanders continuously engage their regional counterparts, such as at the Regional Air Defense Chiefs Conference in November 2013. Engagements such as these allow us to listen to partner nation concerns, assure them of support, and demonstrate U.S. commitment to the region.

We complement operations, exercises, and key leader engagement with efforts aimed at strengthening partner capacity. A key aspect of these initiatives are foreign military sales and foreign military financing programs, including more than $75 billion in U.S. arms sales to Gulf Cooperation Council states since 2007. We are also co-developing advanced ballistic missile defense capabilities with Israel. Additionally, International Military Education and Training is a key investment we are making to build enduring relationships with partner nations, civilian and military leaders. We have trained over 3,000 officers through this program from this region over the last 13 years.

Finally, we are working with partners throughout the region to help them better defend critical assets, including in the physical sense and in the cyber world, including military sites and key infrastructure.

Ladies and gentlemen, your military's men and women are forward deployed every day in the Middle East in support of our national defense. We are proud of their efforts and their sacrifice.

Thank you for this opportunity to speak to your committee this morning, and please accept my gratitude for all you have done for us.

[The prepared statement of Admiral Pandolfe can be found in the Appendix on page 65.]

The CHAIRMAN. Thank you.

As I mentioned in my opening statement, there is a tremendous level of volatility in the Middle East. Last week, we received testimony that Al Qaeda is a growing threat, particularly in Iraq and Syria, and you have referred to that.

Given the failure to achieve a status of forces agreement [SOFA] with Iraq, which could have provided for residual U.S. presence in the region, the rise of Al Qaeda and the associated instability in that region, what lessons can we learn from the experience and how we should transition in Afghanistan?

Ms. SLOTKIN. Okay. Well, obviously, we watch the events going on in Iraq right now very closely. Anyone like myself who served there feels—the only reaction is to feel emotionally when you see what is going on in Anbar.

I do think that the idea that if we had negotiated a follow-on settlement with the Iraqis and had a SOFA and a remaining force, the idea that that force would be able to prevent what is going on is— I am not sure that that would be possible. You know, at the height of the American presence in Iraq, the height of the surge, 170,000 troops, we had levels of violence that we are seeing right now in Anbar, so I am not sure that a remaining force of 10,000 would have been able to prevent this.

More importantly, I do think that our overall goals in the region are to support partners and allies as they manage their own threats, manage threats within their borders. That is our goal in many states in the region, and Iraq being one of them. That is why some of the accelerated weapons transfers that you have been seeing have been going on. We have been pushing very hard to get the Iraqis what they need to take on those threats, learn the lessons that they need to learn to manage those issues within their own territory.

In terms of what it teaches us for Afghanistan, I am not sure the situation is analogous. Back when we were negotiating the original SOFA in 2008, it barely passed the Iraqi parliament on the very last day of the session with a slim margin, and whereas in Afghanistan, you have real support for an enduring presence in the country, both from the loya jirga members, from the members of their parliament, from the average person on the street.

When it came to negotiating a follow-on agreement in 2011 with the Iraqis, the President, our President and Prime Minister Maliki had conversations as two sovereigns, and the prime minister did not believe that he could get a follow-on agreement through his parliament. We respected that decision. And if we couldn't get the protections and immunities that we needed, we weren't going to stay. So I don't think there are direct lessons we can learn for Afghanistan from the Iraq experience, particularly because of the public support in Afghanistan for an enduring presence.

The CHAIRMAN. To what extent is the Department of Defense consulted prior to the United States entering into the interim agreement with Iran regarding its nuclear program?

Ms. SLOTKIN. I am sorry. I misunderstood. The Department of Defense was consulted and involved in the conversations before the agreement was publicized. We were involved in a robust series of interagency conversations.

The CHAIRMAN. Thank you.

Mr. Smith.

Mr. SMITH. Thank you, Mr. Chairman.

I think one of the challenges of the Middle East is balancing our various interests there in terms of, you know, we certainly want stability, and we want to build relationships and have friends. At the same time, we are promoting democracy, we are—this is going into conflict in a number of places, in Egypt most notably, and I think, you know, part of the problem is we set this expectation that we are going to only support democratic and free governments, but it is really not possible. So when you look at Egypt, when you look at Saudi Arabia, when you look at Bahrain and you have some of those challenges where, you know, supporting a government that is not as free and open as we would like them to be is in our best interests in terms of maintaining relationship and stability, I think part of the problem with the credibility of our message is people don't see how we balance those two. We seem to constantly be moving back and forth between the two interests in a way that is confusing for the region.

Now, it is very difficult to balance, but I am just curious how you would say we should go about messaging that and working. And you can get specific in terms of how we should handle Egypt and Saudi Arabia, Bahrain, any of those.

Ambassador PATTERSON. Mr. Smith, this is always a very difficult balancing effort, as you outline. Let me talk for a minute about Egypt. Egypt is a country of 80 million people of enormous strategic importance to the United States and to Israel. We have a longstanding defense relationship with Egypt. We are very concerned about the upsurge in terrorism and insurgency in the Sinai, which is increasingly becoming an ungoverned space, but that said, we are also very concerned about the direction of the government, the arrest of journalists, the crackdown on secular activists. So we do have to balance these interests, and our hope is that we can balance them in an intelligent and effective way by encouraging the government to move toward the democratic process. They seem to be—they had a referendum. They are going to have elections soon, but we have to preserve our national security interests, and we have to preserve our relationship with the Egyptian military, because that is the bulwark of Camp David and in many respects the bulwark of regional peace, so we try to balance these as best we can.

In Bahrain, as you know, there have been a number of discussions, certainly concerns about the human rights situation. We have had many discussions with the government about that, but it is also the home of the 5th Fleet and the center of a very important national security interest in the region. We balance them as best we can. And——

Mr. SMITH. Could we, on that—if I may. Sorry to interrupt. I think part of the problem with the messaging is when we come out, you know, in favor of, you know, a democratic government or opposed to a government because it is not democratic, our language is very strong that this is a core U.S. principle that we will not veer from, and yet everyone in the region knows that we veer from it with great frequency. And I am not saying that is wrong. I mean, you have to make choices; I mean, we cannot imagine perfect governments all around the world. But do you think we sometimes overstate the fact that, you know, come hell or high water, we are going to support democratic governments and then there are just so many obvious examples when we haven't, and is there a way to better balance that message in terms of how people in the region hear it and perceive it?

Ambassador PATTERSON. Certainly, Mr. Smith, after my experience in Egypt, I think our messaging needs work. I would be hard-pressed to say, though, that we should not emphasize our long-term interest in a democratic transition, because that is critically important.

Mr. SMITH. Absolutely.

Ambassador PATTERSON. I mean, they are absolutely—the only way these countries can become stable and prosperous is to move down the democratic path, but, yes, sometimes our messaging is a little in-adroit in all these circumstances.

Mr. SMITH. Thank you. On Syria, in particular, first of all, can you give us your latest assessment of the situation on ground in terms of the extremist groups, Al-Nusra and ISIS [Islamic State of Iraq and Syria]. You know, they seemed to be ascendant for quite some time; slight setbacks a couple weeks ago. How much—where are they at in terms of how dominant they are in the insurgency at this point?

Ambassador PATTERSON. Well, Mr. Smith, they are increasingly important on the battlefield. As I mentioned, there are 7,000 foreign fighters from a large number of countries, including from a large number of Western countries, which means they have Western passports and potentially access to Western countries, but I certainly would not want to rule out the potential for the moderate opposition. Those people are out there fighting and dying every day, but certainly it is of great concern to us that ISIL, Al-Nusra Front and others are—have a seemingly more active role in the battlefield.

There are Islamic groups that we would not call extremists that are being funded by some of our allies. They, too, have a prominent role in the fighting, but yes, it is of great concern to us.

Mr. SMITH. Okay. Anybody else?

Thank you very much. I yield back.

The CHAIRMAN. Thank you.

Mr. Thornberry.

Mr. THORNBERRY. Thank you, Mr. Chairman.

Ambassador Patterson, I want to get back to this subject of credibility that the chairman raised a little bit earlier. And part of what really bothers me is Ms. Slotkin's answer to the chairman's first question. She said essentially that, Well, we—there was a lot of violence in Anbar when—before the surge and so there is really no lesson to be learned there, because our troops wouldn't have made any difference anyway. But what—well, first, of course, there was a tremendous amount of sacrifice that was—of our folks as well as Iraqis required to change the situation in Anbar.

Secondly, the hope was that some sort of continued engagement and advisory would increase their capability and keep them focused on the real enemy, the terrorists, not devolve into sectarian sorts of struggles. And so I want to get—and the fact that we are not there, I kind of wonder does that not affect the—the way the other countries see us as whether we are a reliable partner or not.

Now, that is just kind of preliminary. You, obviously, served next door to Afghanistan. That is something that you have a lot of knowledge and experience about. I would like to hear your view about lessons from Iraq that may apply to Afghanistan and the larger question of U.S. credibility in the Middle East, whether we are a reliable partner or not.

Ambassador PATTERSON. I do think—let me say I do think we are a reliable partner, and I think that our presence is very extensive. Let me just take, for instance, the example of Iraq and what we have done recently. We have made an extraordinary effort with the help of this committee and other committees in the Congress to give them the weaponry and the, frankly, the intelligence support that they need to meet this renewed threat from ISIL. And it was critically important that we provided Hellfire missiles, because they had attempted to go after these camps in the desert with thin-skinned helicopters and with—by ground, and had been unable to do so, so our armament came in at a critical point to enable them to go after some of these terrorists.

We also have tried to step up training, we are planning to step up training. We have an enormous foreign military sales and foreign military financing program with Iraq. So I think it is very difficult to say that we have abandoned the Iraqis, because I think we are very intensely engaged there.

And as to your broader question, sir, yes, I think we are going to need to be involved in these countries, whether it is Afghanistan or Pakistan or Iraq or Egypt, for decades to come, and not just in the military sense. The key element in all these countries is going to be job creation for the enormous number of young men that are coming into the labor force and basically have no prospects are a built-in element of instability. So, yes, generally speaking, whether it is by troops or through assistance or through our investment programs or any number of other mechanisms, we are going to have to be in these countries in force for decades to come.

Mr. THORNBERRY. Well, I would just say I hope that the situation in Afghanistan does not have to get as bad and deteriorate as much as it had—as it did in Iraq before we re-engaged. It got—well, secondly, I hear what you are saying and you all are all, you know, stating your opinion about our credibility, but I will just say what I hear from a variety of countries and U.S. people who visit those countries is they have real doubts about the U.S. position, whether we are a reliable ally; part of it is the negotiations with Iran, part of it is the pivot to Asia, part of it is our unclear policy with Egypt and Syria. And my fear is that doubts about our credibility increase the dangers in that region, and nothing would cause that to be in greater doubt than for us to abandon Afghanistan in the same way we did in Iraq.

So thank you. I yield back.

The CHAIRMAN. Thank you.

Ms. Davis.

Mrs. DAVIS. Thank you, Mr. Chairman.

Thank you all for being with us today.

Admiral, if I could just start with you for a second, because I—we talked about the Pacific pivot certainly in this committee, and I am wondering—you also spoke certainly about a number of exercises in the region and I appreciate that, but I wonder how you assess our security goals, how they would be affected if our Navy was reduced in the total number of ships, including an aircraft carrier, of course, and also some of the LCS [littoral combat ship] fleet. Is that—where does that fit into the discussion?

Admiral PANDOLFE. Well, when the service chiefs come up, they attest to the requirements of their services, as derived from analytical analysis, which includes contingency planning, and the Chief of Naval Operations has testified to the size of the Navy that he feels is most appropriate and asked for funding for that fleet. We are concerned with the size of the Navy today, and we ask for your support to try to meet the Chief of Naval Operations' requirements.

Mrs. DAVIS. Do you pick up from our partners in the region that the discussion of the Pacific shift, pivot, is of concern to them?

Admiral PANDOLFE. I don't think it is of tremendous concern. I think we have to—we have to explain the context, which is that in a rising Asia economically, it is important that we stay engaged in that theater, and that much of the rebalance we are talking about is the flow of forces that had been surged into Iraq and Afghanistan now returning to their normal bases in Hawaii and Washington State and Okinawa.

It is by no means a disengagement from the Middle East. We have made that very, very clear. We retain extraordinary forces in the Middle East, not just quantitatively, but qualitatively, and we are fully prepared to meet our security commitments.

As mentioned in my statements and others, our leadership continually passes this message personally to the leadership in that area, and I think they understand that and they do believe that we will be there for a long time to come in the numbers and the capabilities needed.

Mrs. DAVIS. Thank you. I appreciate that.

Madam Ambassador and Ms. Slotkin, actually, it remains a big deal, I think, to all of us that you are here testifying together. There was a long time before sometimes that occurred, and I wonder if you could share with us, in the midst of so many issues, crises, obviously, in the Middle East, how your Departments are prioritizing, synchronizing means to achieve a unity of effort. What can you point to that is really different? And I wonder in that discussion if you could also focus on the actual threats to the United States. We know that there are continual crises within the region, but focus on the threats to the United States particularly.

Ambassador PATTERSON. Thank you. We have, in answer to your first question, extremely close collaboration with DOD. Frankly, it is as close as I have seen it in many respects in my 40-year career. For instance, when General Austin went out to the Gulf a few weeks ago, essentially to reassure our allies, Brett McGurk, who is very knowledgeable about Iraq, went with him. We have many such joint efforts and many meetings and collaboration on issues like our military assistance to Egypt and every other country. There is an extraordinary degree of collaboration, if I might say so, a very amiable relationship, which also wasn't always the case, but is certainly the case now.

And on threats to the United States, I think when General Clapper testified last week, I think there is, of course, growing concern about the global reach of some of the groups that are operating in Syria right now, and the movement of some of the more hardened terrorists from the tribal areas of Pakistan into Syria who might potentially pose a threat to the United States.

Mrs. DAVIS. Thank you.

Ms. Slotkin, would you——

Ms. SLOTKIN. Sure. I couldn't agree more. Certainly, as someone who worked on the Middle East, in terms of the cooperation among the interagency, I would characterize my experience in the previous administration as pretty adversarial. Now, maybe between agencies, maybe that was because I was working on Iraq, and it was particularly political, but it is the tone of the conversation I think has fundamentally changed, and while we meet with our interagency colleagues on a daily basis, it is the tone to me that is the most important change, not just the frequency of meetings. We work on everything together, so I think that that is a positive thing.

In terms of the threats, obviously, we look at the threats coming out of Syria, Al-Nusra Front and the terrorists and extremist groups that are powerful there. And I think one of the positive examples of interagency collaboration has been our approach to dealing with containment of that threat in particular, so we have, in the past, I would say, year really upped our game with Jordan, what we are doing in Jordan. So in addition to the Patriots and the F–16s we have there, we have a military presence that supports increased border activity, helping the Jordanians train to manage threats to their borders. The same thing with Lebanon. We have a robust program with the Lebanese armed forces, but recently with the help, frankly, of the Congress, have moved ahead on some border security, additional border security programs dealing with——

——

The CHAIRMAN. Thank you.

Ms. SLOTKIN [continuing]. The Lebanese——

The CHAIRMAN. The lady's time has expired.

Ms. SLOTKIN. Pardon.

The CHAIRMAN. Mr. Forbes.

Mr. FORBES. Thank you, Mr. Chairman.

And thank all of you for being here. I would like to continue this question that the chairman began and Mr. Thornberry had about credibility.

And, Ms. Slotkin, it seems like I heard you say that—if I didn't misunderstand, that we will not allow Iran to get a nuclear weapon, and you said that without any qualification at all. Is that correct?

Ms. SLOTKIN. Correct. That is our current policy, yes.

Mr. FORBES. Let me ask you this, then, because we do have some credibility problems. In fact, when you just made the mention of the previous administration was more adversarial, to some of us, we feel like maybe the Department of Defense was standing up a little bit more to State, and sometimes you are not adversarial if you are just saying, Okay, we will go along with what you want to do.

But I look, and this administration could not stop a single employee of a nongovernment contractor from stealing and distributing to the world some of the most vital military secrets of this Nation, secrets that many members of this committee wouldn't have even had security clearance to look at. And yet you sit there and tell us, without qualification, that we will not allow Iran to get a nuclear weapon. Isn't it true that we may not even know when they are close to having a nuclear weapon?

Ms. SLOTKIN. So what I would say is the President has stated over and over again——

Mr. FORBES. I understand what the President has stated.

Ms. SLOTKIN. Okay. So, to your issue first of credibility, so this strategy is——

Mr. FORBES. No, no. If you don't mind, you have stated there unequivocally that we will not allow them to get a nuclear weapon, and yet you have heard and we have seen what has happened, even within the protection of our own information. How can you guarantee this committee that you are even going to know when Iran is close to having a nuclear weapon?

Ms. SLOTKIN. Sir, particularly in an unclassified forum, the most I will say is General Clapper was up on the Hill talking about the Intelligence Community assessment, and we believe that should Iran make the decision to pursue a nuclear weapon, that we—it would take at least a year for them to do that. We can talk additionally in a classified forum, but for this forum, you know, the DNI [Director of National Intelligence] has said this clearly. Obviously the Department of Defense supports that assessment. That is our best estimation based on the intelligence we have.

Mr. FORBES. And I don't have a problem saying it is our best guess, best estimation. It is when you come in here and say that the tack you are taking, unequivocally we are going to keep Iran from getting a nuclear weapon, I think that puts in jeopardy your credibility for being able to say that, because if we guess wrong, if the President guesses wrong in the direction he is going, we may not even know that until it is too late.

But, Admiral, let me shift, if I can, to you. One of the things that I would like to ask you, Admiral, what regional initiatives both unilaterally and multilaterally are being undertaken to deal with growing Iranian anti-access/area denial [A2/AD] capabilities? How can the U.S. stiffen Gulf State resolve to resist Iranian belligerence in the event of a conflict to maintain U.S. access to forward bases, and what lessons or synergies can be gleaned from our attempts to preserve American power projection in the Asia-Pacific to assist our efforts in the Persian Gulf area?

Admiral PANDOLFE. So there are a number of initiatives to address the A2/AD threat that Iran poses in the Gulf and to its neighbors. So——

The CHAIRMAN. Admiral, could you pull that mike up, sir?

Admiral PANDOLFE. I am sorry.

The CHAIRMAN. Thank you.

Admiral PANDOLFE. There are a number of initiatives that we are working to help counter the Iranian A2/AD threat. Among them are working with the Israelis on ballistic missile defense programs, including their suite of weapons, which are coming along very well, and integrating the Gulf States into a more comprehensive air and missile defense architecture. This was discussed by Secretary Hagel recently in his overseas speech in Manama. We are working to train forces in a number of countries for border security and for counterterrorism to get at the—in the terrorist threat sponsored by the Iranian threat network.

So when you look at the array of capabilities from conventional ballistic missile all the way down to sea denial and then into the—in the asymmetric or terrorist world, we are sponsoring programs to strengthen our friends and partners, as mentioned by Ms. Slotkin, both bilaterally and increasingly multilaterally, to put down a clear marker that these nations are united in their concern about and their intention to push back against Iranian attempts at intimidation.

For our own Nation, we are——

Mr. FORBES. And, Admiral, my time is up.

Admiral PANDOLFE. I am sorry, sir.

Mr. FORBES. But maybe I can chat with you a little bit more at a later time, but thank you so much for that information.

Mr. Chairman, I yield back.

The CHAIRMAN. Thank you.

Mr. Langevin.

Mr. LANGEVIN. Thank you, Mr. Chairman.

I would like to thank our witnesses for being here today. Let me—I have several questions that I would like to get to. Let me start with one with respect to ISIL.

Last week, we saw an unprecedented move from Al Qaeda's leadership to disassociate themselves from ISIL. What does this latest move mean for the strategy of core Al Qaeda going forward and specifically for their influence and abilities within the geopolitical landscape of the Middle East? And has this announcement affected our approach to fighting Al Qaeda?

Ms. SLOTKIN. Obviously, we watched Zawahiri's announcement with great interest in the government since it was the first time we have seen an affiliate actually have a break with Al Qaeda central. I think we are still trying to assess exactly what it means in terms of your question on impact on sort of regional policy, and I think one of the fundamental questions we have is, is this a sign of strength or a sign of weakness for Al Qaeda core?

Certainly, I think our early initial—our early assessments indicate that it means that Al Qaeda core is very interested in what happens in Syria. Right? So ISIL had been accused by Al Qaeda core of insubordination, and ISIL has obviously become very powerful in Iraq in addition to Syria.

One possibility that we are still exploring is that the Al Qaeda core is more interested in Syria than anything else in the region and has put their emphasis on Al-Nusra Front because of the importance of Syria. We are still trying to assess what it means for our policies, and we watch it very, very closely.

Mr. LANGEVIN. And with respect to the ISIL demonstrating insubordination, as Zawahiri called it, what was the center of that insubordination? What is it that they are referring to?

Ms. Slotkin. I think, again, in an unclassified forum, they had good old-fashioned command and control problems——

Mr. Langevin. Okay.

Ms. Slotkin [continuing]. Listening to the boss.

Mr. Langevin. Okay, thanks.

Turning to Egypt, what are the United States policy objectives with regards to Egypt over the short and the long term, and let's start with that.

Ambassador Patterson. Thank you.

The policy objectives are to promote a democratic transition, and Egypt has had a referendum. Again, it was not problem-free, but there are elections, and then to promote our national security interests which involve our longstanding relationship with the Egyptian military which goes back many decades and to do everything possible we can to help the Egyptians reduce some of the terrorists and insurgency in the Sinai.

We are working with the Egyptian military. We have continued counterterrorism cooperation, we have continued sustainment, we have continued training to help them meet these new threats. So we have really multifaceted objectives in Egypt.

Mr. Langevin. And right now, how do you assess how stable the Egyptian economy is and are their foreign currency reserves and the external assistance they receive, are they adequate to meet their needs?

Ambassador Patterson. Almost certainly not, Congressman. They have gotten an influx of foreign exchange from the Gulf countries to the tune of somewhere around $10 billion and that has shored them up, but Egypt has been very hard hit by the decline in tourism and the freezing essentially of investment flows, and it is essential that Egypt undertake some economic reforms and get some political stability so it can realize really the enormous economic future that it has before them. But the situation is rather dire at the moment.

Mr. Langevin. And worst case, what could we reasonably expect with regards to the governance situation in the country if the Egyptian economy collapses?

Ambassador Patterson. Well, certainly in my view their economic problems were key in these periodic upheavals, and again the huge unemployment, particularly among young men. If they don't solve their economic problems and they don't find jobs for all these people coming into the labor force, we are going to continue to see political instability and street demonstration and threats to the governments that are unable to meet the goals of their people.

Mr. Langevin. And what is at stake right now with respect to the next round of Egyptian elections and are there any possible outcomes likely to lead to the denigration in the security situation?

Ambassador Patterson. Well, the security situation has deteriorated recently with the increase in activity of a Ansar Beit al-Maqdis. It is a group that has only been active in the Sinai. So there has been some considerable deterioration. We are hopeful that the referendum, the presidential elections, and now the parliamentary elections will bring some political stability to Egypt that will then allow the economy to get back on its feet.

The Chairman. Thank you.

The gentleman's time expired.

Mr. Conaway.

Mr. CONAWAY. Thank you, Mr. Chairman, and I thank the witnesses for being here and your long service to our country.

Ms. Slotkin, I too was struck by the declarative statement that you made that Iran will not get a nuclear weapon. This administration has at least from a domestic standpoint, has got some pretty famous declarative statements out there that haven't really worked all that well. You had nothing to do with that and I got that. So if they snuck up on us and got one, would you also interpret that to say we would not let them keep it?

Ms. SLOTKIN. Yes. So I think the President has been very clear on this that——

Mr. CONAWAY. His credibility is not real good with us; what is your thinking on this?

Ms. SLOTKIN. So I think what is frankly underwriting the current work on diplomacy on this issue is the Department of Defense's strong posture in the region and our ability to act from that posture against——

Mr. CONAWAY. Okay.

Ms. SLOTKIN [continuing]. All contingencies, and, frankly, our——

Mr. CONAWAY. Okay. But your recommendation is that we would not let them keep a weapon. If you are committed to them not getting one, and I assume you are, you made the statement——

Ms. SLOTKIN. Of course.

Mr. CONAWAY. Your recommendation is we would not let them keep it either, right?

Ms. SLOTKIN. All options are on the table.

Mr. CONAWAY. Okay.

Ms. SLOTKIN. The President has said that and the Department of Defense is——

Mr. CONAWAY. All right, let me pivot to Russia and the influence they are having in Egypt, Syria, and other places. Madam Ambassador, what are your thoughts. Are they being helpful in the region, hurtful, and what do you think Putin is trying to do?

Ambassador PATTERSON. Well, Congressman, it is a mix. I mean they have been helpful in the P5+1 [U.N. Security Council permanent members plus Germany] negotiations with Iran, they have been helpful in the quartet, they have been helpful in the removal of Syria's chemical weapons, and my own view is, for instance, their so-called inroads into Egypt are much exaggerated. I mean we have a very robust and longstanding relationship with Egypt on the military side. There is some residual Russian equipment and there were some trips there by Russian officials, but again, I don't think it they can begin to compete with our relationship with the Egyptian military.

Mr. CONAWAY. And your assessment that keeping Assad in power in Syria is in Russia's best interest?

Ambassador PATTERSON. That is a difficult question, Congressman. I think the Russians are conflicted and, well, I think they are very concerned about the terrorist—the growth in terrorism in Syria which threatens their own country. There are a number of Chechens there. And this is a subject of constant interaction with the Secretary and other officials with the Russian government. We are trying to work very closely with them. We have managed to do so on chemical weapons, and we are trying to work very closely with them on humanitarian access and on the broader picture.

Mr. CONAWAY. All right. Madam Ambassador, I was also piqued by your comment that the United States would have some role in creating jobs in these countries. Again, the administration that serves us right now has got a very poor track record of creating jobs here in America for our youth and young men and women trying to come into this workforce. Do you really see us—as that being one of our core roles, is to create jobs in these countries?

Ambassador PATTERSON. Actually I do. You know, we can act as catalyst on job creation. It is not the U.S. Government that creates jobs, it is American companies and foreign investors that create jobs and the local people that create jobs. But we can do things like promote programs on entrepreneurship, like promote innovation, like promote high schools in technology and science. There are things we can do through our assistance programs that can facilitate that.

Mr. CONAWAY. Okay.

Ambassador PATTERSON. Yes, I do think we have a role.

Mr. CONAWAY. So, could we morph some of the domestic policies this administration has been unsuccessful with over the last 5 years to use as the guideposts in your part of the world?

Ambassador PATTERSON. Well, I just mentioned, Congressman, a few of the projects I think we can do and have done successfully in this part of the world to facilitate investment. It is the private sector and it needs to play a greater role.

Mr. CONAWAY. Okay, well, I appreciate that clarification. It is the private sector. Madam Ambassador, I was whacking at you a little bit. I honor your service. You have been in the worst parts of the world for a long time, so, please don't—I am trying not to be disrespectful, but you have got a bad hand to play. But you have been in a bad part of the world for a long part of your career and I really respect that immensely.

Mr. Chairman, I yield back.

The CHAIRMAN. Thank you.

Mr. Johnson.

Mr. JOHNSON. Thank you, Mr. Chairman.

I think if we listen to the comments of my brothers and some sisters on the other side of the aisle we will come to the conclusion that the Obama administration is responsible for every problem that America has, both domestically and internationally, and it is a shame I think that we have now come to politicization of our foreign policy partisanship on that issue.

The issues that we deal with on this committee are much too complex and serious than to devolve into partisanship on this committee, and I think our history as a nation has brought us to this point, and that has not been a partisan issue, and it is going to take all of us to work towards a more peaceful and prosperous world. I don't think there is anybody out here that doesn't want peace and prosperity, and that is what we should be fighting for, that is what we should be employing our hard power to produce when it is necessary, and we should also be focusing so much on our soft power that can actually produce the peaceful result.

And I think that there has been a lot of success that this administration can claim in terms of peaceful progress, and I won't go over all of them, from reaching an agreement with Iran for a 6-month period to navigating an agreement to prevent them from becoming a nuclear weapons power, to the removal of—or the march towards the removal of chemical weapons from Syria, the extraction of our forces from the unfortunate war in Iraq, and unfortunately for them and for us, they did not enable us to sign a status of forces agreement over there so we had to come on out, and the same thing will happen in Afghanistan if they don't agree to the very reasonable terms of a status of forces agreement.

So I would like to ask though about Egypt and the fact that there are at least 23 journalists who have been arrested and charged with terrorism or support of terrorism due to the fact that they have been reporting on the Muslim Brotherhood. I would like for you to speak on, Ambassador Patterson, our efforts, if any, to produce the freedom for those journalists. Indeed, if Egypt is to become a nation with democratic ideals, it should certainly start with freedom of the press which is closely linked to freedom of association and freedom of speech.

Can you give us, Ambassador Patterson, some idea on America's way forward in ensuring that those journalists can be freed?

Ambassador PATTERSON. Yes, thank you, Congressman.

We entirely agree with your assessment that freedom of the press is absolutely key because it surfaces all the other issues. Let me assure you, Congressman, that the administration has pressed hard on this issue.

It has been the subject of Secretary Kerry's conversations with Egyptian leaders, it has been the subject of Secretary Hagel's conversation was his counterparts in Egypt, and we will continue to press on these issues and urge that these journalists be released. A number of them are non-Egyptian. Some of them are very distinguished in their field. It is hard to believe they were reporting unfairly, and even if they had been that is most certainly not a grounds for their arrest.

But it is a very high priority for us, as is encouraging the Egyptian government to enable freedom of association, and they have some recent laws which have curtailed that as well. These are worrisome trends, sir.

The CHAIRMAN. Thank you very much. The gentleman's time has expired.

Mr. Lamborn.

Mr. LAMBORN. Thank you, Mr. Chairman.

This is for either for Secretary Slotkin or Ambassador Patterson. I am concerned that in Iran we have not known everything that was going on until sometimes years after the fact—years after the fact. The secret facility at Qom, for instance, we didn't know about that for years.

So Secretary Slotkin, when you say it would be a year from when they would try to start breaking out and develop a nuclear weapon from their current status, and yet I know that we have allies and others like our Israeli allies and others who think it would be as little as 2 months, but whatever it is, whether it is closer to 2 months or closer to 12 months, is the U.S. military prepared to act in that limited window and use force if that is what it would take to keep Iran from actually deploying a nuclear weapon?

Ms. SLOTKIN. Sure. So just starting from the top, first on the interim deal, first of all the joint plan of action allows for the IAEA [International Atomic Energy Agency] to verify Iran's compliance with the deal. I understand you are talking about there if there are things that are not on the table, but certainly the IAEA has a role until verifying compliance now. Any comprehensive agreement that we ever negotiate will emphasize verifiable means, right? We will have to have solid proof, we will not rely on just trusting the Iranians. And then, importantly, we remain confident that we could tell if Iran was making a dash towards a weapon and we believe should that decision be made, it would take at least a year.

I stand by that, and I think in an unclassified forum that is as far as I will go. If for some reason negotiations broke down, if we didn't get a comprehensive deal, the President said all options are on the table, and the Department of Defense is prepared to take any action that the President deems——

Mr. LAMBORN. Okay, let me follow up on that for either you or the Ambassador, and this has already been alluded to by Mr. Thornberry and Mr. Forbes and others. But the credibility issue, I see that the lack of action in Syria, whether or not it would have been right for the U.S. to step in and use force to punish the use of chemical weapons upon his own people by Bashar Assad, the fact is that the Iranians are viewing that as a lack of credibility and a sign of weakness.

What indications do we have that the Iranians are really taking seriously the threat that the U.S. would act militarily? I think that the credibility gap has widened considerably and is a very troubling thing.

Ambassador PATTERSON. Congressman, I think one issue that we sort of overlooked here is their economy is in shreds. The sanctions have been extraordinarily effective in reducing their access to international financial institutions and reducing their petroleum production. So that has clearly gotten their attention and brought them to the table to negotiate.

Mr. LAMBORN. But has that been undone now to a large extent? I hear there is what is called a gold rush of European countries and the private sector going into Iran and now saying that they are open for business.

Ambassador PATTERSON. Congressman, let me stress that Iran is not open for business and the American government will do everything it possibly can to enforce these sanctions on any company that would be so unwise as to engage in business with Iran right now. Yes, they are going, and I hope they are giving the message to Iran that if we were able to do business with you, there would be advantages. That is putting more pressure on them.

But please rest assured that the sanctions have been effective, gotten them to the table. I don't think the credibility issue, again it seems that economically Iran is in a very weak position right now. So I think the issue of credibility, I do think, yes, some people would complain about that, but I think we are engaged militarily, we have gotten Iran to the table, we have an enormously robust presence in the Gulf and elsewhere in the region, so it is hard for me to see that our credibility has eroded.

Mr. LAMBORN. Admiral, let me ask one really fast question of you.

We have sold arms, advanced arms, to some of the countries in the region outside of Israel. Are we able to make sure that they comply with the restrictions on the use of those advanced weaponry and arms?

Admiral PANDOLFE. Yes. First of all, before we agree to those arms sales, it goes through a very thorough vetting process to make sure that the qualitative military edge considerations are fully acknowledged and accepted in terms of ensuring there is a strategic balance that is properly maintained. Then we do have end-user agreement specifics in the agreements which allow us to make sure that the weapons are being employed to the role and mission that they were intended.

Mr. LAMBORN. Thank you.

The CHAIRMAN. Thank you.

Ms. Hanabusa.

Ms. HANABUSA. Thank you, Mr. Chairman.

Admiral, you testified about the Eagle Resolve as well as Eager Lion and there is a reference to 12 and 19 countries respectively that have participated in that. Can you give me an idea of who these countries are?

Admiral PANDOLFE. I would have to go back to CENTCOM to get the specific list, ma'am. I will be happy to forward them to you. Generally, I am most familiar actually with the third example which is the International Mine Countermeasure exercise. And that involved a lot of nations from the region, it also involved NATO allies, and I believe there was even some nations from the Far East. But I can get you the specific lists of which nations participated in each exercise.

Ms. HANABUSA. Well, do you know off the top of your head which countries from the Middle East participated in these exercises?

Admiral PANDOLFE. Generally they are the Gulf States, and I would have to check whether Saudi Arabia participated or not.

Ms. HANABUSA. So if you could forward that to me, to the committee and the committee will forward it, I would really appreciate it.

Admiral PANDOLFE. Yes, ma'am.

[The information referred to can be found in the Appendix on page 73.]

Ms. HANABUSA. Madam Ambassador, in reading your testimony, of course that is where we have the reference to ISIL as well as there is also the "L" is Levant or however you may pronounce it. And I also see that reference in terms of Syria, and I understand it is some kind of a geographical reference. But why is it now appearing in like ISIL and the reference to Syria. Is there any significance in the use of that word?

Ambassador PATTERSON. Well, yes, because I think they have changed or rather expanded their focus to include Syria and—to include Syria. So it is not just Iraq anymore.

Ms. HANABUSA. But doesn't it also geographically include Israel and other countries?

Ambassador PATTERSON. Yes, ma'am.

Ms. HANABUSA. So what is the significance of now referring to the context, like Iraq, for example, to have itself referred to with Levant at the end?

Ambassador PATTERSON. Well, I think it refers to their aspirations to expand throughout the region. And let me say that is one reason we are working very intensely with Syria's neighbors, Jordan and Lebanon, in particular, the King is here this week and I am sure he will be talking to members of the committee, to shore up their counterterrorism capabilities and to improve the control of their borders.

Ms. HANABUSA. So is it a correct statement to say that by the inclusion of this word that they are sort of asserting a different jurisdiction? Because my understanding is that it includes Cyprus, Palestine territories, the Palestinian territories, Israel, Jordan, Lebanon, and Syria, for example, that that is traditionally what it was. So are they somehow by calling themselves ISIL, Syria and Levant, saying this is really the region that we control or should control?

Ambassador PATTERSON. I think that would be right, Congresswoman, that they have a vision of greater expansion. Yes.

Ms. HANABUSA. So how does that play in with Israel being part of that, that area that they perceive to be within their territorial expansion?

Ambassador PATTERSON. Well, let me stress that as far as I am aware, we have not seen any activity by this group in Israel, although Israel, of course, is the subject of security threats from elsewhere in the region. But I certainly—so let me just say that I would go back to what Ms. Slotkin said, that Israel's security is one of our highest national priorities and we will do everything possible we can to work with the Israelis to shore up their defenses and to share intelligence, I wanted to go back to that, to share intelligence on the broad range of threats in the region.

Ms. HANABUSA. So do we as a country, when we agree to refer to Iraq, for example, ISIL, or we allow them to continue or we defer or we give them the credibility of using it in terms of their description of who they are now, are we somehow encouraging it or conceding just simply by the fact that, for example, it is found in your testimony, it is found in other references; are we giving some ground by doing that versus saying no, you are not going to refer to yourself that way?

Ambassador PATTERSON. I wouldn't think so, Congresswoman. I would think we were just sort of recognizing the facts of the matter on that. They are a more expansive organization than they have been in the past and I think we are merely recognizing that fact.

Ms. HANABUSA. But it is not an organization that everyone who is a member of is conceding that their membership within that group?

Ambassador PATTERSON. No, certainly the countries involved. But the organization itself has a more aspirational—it is spreading, I think, to be blunt about it.

The CHAIRMAN. Thank you.

Mr. Scott.

Mr. SCOTT. Thank you, Mr. Chairman.

Ambassador Patterson, you made the statement that we are going to be in these countries in force for decades to come a little while ago. Can you tell me specifically which countries you are talking about and what type of force you are talking about in that statement?

Ambassador PATTERSON. Well, Congressman, I think it is not just military force, it is also economic force. I mean, we took down our flag in Afghanistan in 1989 and literally moved out. There was a lot going on elsewhere in the world, but it is not just our military force that matters, it is our investors, it is our educators, it is our assistance programs, and we are going to require very robust engagement by all elements of U.S. national power in these countries to stabilize them.

Mr. SCOTT. Which countries specifically are you talking about?

Ambassador PATTERSON. We can speak about almost any one of them, but let me take Egypt because I recently left Egypt. We are going to require—we are going to have to have American investment there, we are going to have to have a robust trade relationship, we are going to have to increase educational exchanges. There are only 3,000 Egyptian students in the United States. I think that is an embarrassment. So we want more educational activity, just for an example.

So there are many ways we can engage with these countries that go beyond our military presence and in the long run are frankly just as important.

Mr. SCOTT. I guess when we talk about these other countries, it is not that I question your abilities or the Secretary, or our abilities as a country to help things as much as I question our capacity and the capacity of the United States economy. If every dollar that we spend in interest on the national debt is a dollar that is going to come out of discretionary spending.

And so I guess my next question would be for Secretary Slotkin. The DOD, we are involved in a lot of countries and a lot of conflicts, you are taking a lot of cuts in the Department of Defense. Do you think that you have the capacity based on the budget that you have today to carry out the mission for decades to come?

Ms. SLOTKIN. I do. I mean, I would say to the Ambassador's point that the bilateral relationships that we have are the cornerstones of our approach in the region, and frankly the investment we make up in front in training their military, their security forces, and military education and civ-mil relations pays big dividends for us later on in preventing conflict, preventing spill-out of extremist groups, you name it.

So I feel like the relatively small amount of money frankly that we spend on some of the programs the Ambassador is talking about that we do in non-conflict situations prevents the significantly more expensive operations, combat situations that we are still dealing with.

So I do think that we are positioning. Frankly, you know, it won't be long enough until we have released our QDR [Quadrennial Defense Review] and you will see an enhanced focus on the importance of partnership and training ahead of a problem, building partner capacity ahead of a problem.

Mr. SCOTT. Admiral, if I am correct in reading the Treasury's reports and where our money is going, we are spending more money in interest on the national debt than we are in military pay for our men and women in uniform. The projections are that those interest payments are going to continue to escalate at a fairly rapid pace. Any dollar that is paid in interest comes out of discretionary spending. Obviously the DOD gets about 50 percent of that.

Again, do you have the equipment, the men, and the men that you need to protect this Nation?

Admiral PANDOLFE. Yes, sir. Today absolutely we do, and, as mentioned, particularly in this area, in the Asia-Pacific we are focusing our best resources. As we move forward we are going to have to be very careful to ensure that we maintain the capabilities and capacity that we need by making wise choices with investments.

Mr. SCOTT. I would respectfully submit that the lack of investment right now in equipment and technology and the things that we are going to need to fight the battles that we are going to be in going forward, that maybe we should concentrate more on the United States than some of these countries.

And quite honestly, Ambassador, if a country doesn't respect a person's religious freedom, if the leadership of a country doesn't trust their own people with religious freedom, then I don't see why we should think that we can trust the leadership of that country.

Thank you.

The CHAIRMAN. Thank you.

Mr. Courtney.

Mr. COURTNEY. Thank you, Mr. Chairman, and thank you for holding this hearing and the witnesses for being here this morning.

We have heard, you know, a lot of talk in the back and forth about lessons learned and whether or not in particularly the case of Iraq and as far as our credibility whether or not Iraq was abandoned. I think that was one of the statements that was made here.

You know, one of the lessons that I certainly think we should reflect on was the statement by Secretary Gates, who is hardly an apologist for this administration as we have seen in recent weeks, that any Secretary of Defense who advises a U.S. President to get involved in a ground war in the Middle East ought to have their head examined.

And so, you know, Ms. Slotkin, when the questions were posed to you earlier about Iraq and whether or not our credibility has somehow been damaged because of events that flowed since 2011, I mean you were intimately involved based on your résumé with the transition that took place.

And again, just to reiterate the point, because we had a number of hearings in this committee about the status of forces agreement negotiations. Again, the reason why the final outcome occurred was because of this issue of immunity of prosecution for our troops staying there.

So, in other words, if a soldier from Norwich, Connecticut, without an immunity provision, you know, got picked up by the Iraqi military police or even civilian police, basically they were completely exposed to the criminal justice system or the military justice system of that country, which was unacceptable to both the Bush administrations and the Obama administration.

I mean is that a correct accounting of the back and forth that took place?

Ms. SLOTKIN. I think it is correct to say that regardless of administration, there are certain basic SOFA provisions, and trying our own people in our own courts is a basic tenet of any SOFA negotiation around the world.

The Bush administration wasn't going to let our soldiers be exposed to the Iraqi courts and neither was the Obama administration. I don't believe that was the only issue. We certainly had a very complicated recent past with Iraqis, but that certainly was one issue.

Mr. COURTNEY. Certainly in this committee, and I recall those hearings well, I mean that was a very bright line as far as any agreement moving forward.

Ms. SLOTKIN. It was the single most difficult part of the original SOFA to negotiate. I was on the original team and it came down to the last couple of months and it was the single most controversial issue of the original SOFA signed back in 2008.

Mr. COURTNEY. And, again, as far as the other side of that negotiation, again it was a pretty adamant provision of the Iraqi negotiators, that they insisted on it, and in fact I believe there was even a vote in the Iraqi parliament that took place again sort of reiterating that position. I may not have that totally correct. But the bottom line is that it is important for people to remember that this didn't happen in a vacuum. That kind of comes with the territory when you are doing bilateral negotiations and you are fostering democracy and some of these things. Their position, you know, affects the outcome of negotiations.

And Ambassador, you I know have a history in Afghanistan. I mean this issue of immunity from prosecution actually is not a stumbling block right now. I mean that is something that at least press reports suggest, the two sides have actually agreed on that. There is other issues that are hindering a completion of the agreement. But, again, just as an example, it is sort of a contrast, I mean how important that is.

Well, again, maybe, Ms. Slotkin, you can——

Ms. SLOTKIN. Sure. I mean this is a fundamental difference between where we were with Iraq in 2011 and where we are now with Afghanistan is that the people of Afghanistan, the parliamentarians of Afghanistan, the members of the loya jirga, they support an enduring presence.

And we just didn't have the same facts on the ground in 2011 in Iraq for a whole variety of reasons. And I think that you are right, we largely have the contours of an agreement, we just need the political will to get it signed, and we urge President Karzai to sign it as soon as possible.

Mr. COURTNEY. Great. Thank you.

Ambassador, you have mentioned the efforts in Syria to remove the chemical weapons and again there has been some progress with the production facilities. You know, there was an interesting report that we had about the U.S. Navy's participation in this process that they have actually got a container ship ready to go, the USS *Ray*.

And again, I was wondering if you could just sort of talk about the fact that, again, we have to get the pace moving, but the fact is, is that our military is doing an outstanding job in terms of getting this, in my opinion, great accomplishment completed.

Ambassador PATTERSON. Yes, Congressman. This is really an important advance. It was the biggest threat to the most number of Syrians, and, importantly, it was the biggest threat to Syria's neighbors as well. So it was very important to address this issue.

The removal has stalled and we are doing everything we can to push the Syrians to remove the weapons as soon as possible. It has been a great example of international cooperation. But it is important to realize too that the machines which actually make the materials, mix the materials, have already been removed, so Syria's capacity to actually deploy a chemical weapon is very, very greatly reduced.

The CHAIRMAN. Thank you.

Mr. Cook.

Mr. COOK. Thank you, Mr. Chair.

I have got a number of questions so I might cut off the speakers and I will apologize in advance.

Admiral, first of all, real quick on MRAPs [Mine Resistant Ambush Protected vehicles] and the situation in Fallujah, Anbar Province, and everything else, that it is not just the helicopters, it is also the fact that IEDs [improvised explosive devices] are a big problem. We had a committee hearing that said they are going to chop up a number of them that are coming out of Afghanistan. I wonder if this might be one of the carrots that we could use with the Maliki government. I don't trust his government, particularly the relations with Iran. If you could briefly comment on that.

Admiral PANDOLFE. My understanding is that we are not cutting up the MRAPs as was previously discussed.

Mr. COOK. That policy has changed?

The CHAIRMAN. Admiral.

Admiral PANDOLFE. Yes, I will go back and check on that, but my understanding is that has changed.

Mr. COOK. Because we——

Admiral PANDOLFE. Yes.

Mr. COOK [continuing]. Were briefed, and it wasn't that long ago——

Admiral PANDOLFE. Yes, sir.

Mr. COOK [continuing]. And I am there as, you know, a dumb grunt——

Admiral PANDOLFE. Right.

Mr. COOK [continuing]. That always took his equipment out saying, what in God's—we spent all this money and everything like that and okay——

Admiral PANDOLFE. I believe we have revisited that, and let me go back and double-check that for you.

Mr. COOK. Okay.

Admiral PANDOLFE. Regarding the Iraqis, we are responding to the lists of capabilities that they have given us. They have told us what they think they need to recapture the areas that are contested.

Mr. COOK. Particularly Fallujah?

Admiral PANDOLFE. Yes, sir.

Mr. COOK. And when they have tried, they have really gotten whacked pretty bad, haven't they?

Admiral PANDOLFE. I don't want to comment on what their——

Mr. COOK. Okay.

Admiral PANDOLFE [continuing]. Operational plans are. But they have given us a list of the capabilities they feel they need and we are moving swiftly to provide those.

Mr. COOK. Okay, could I switch to the Ambassadors real quick, on the Kurds. We haven't heard much about the Kurds. I know they have the pipeline, things are looking better, obviously tremendous in regards to their economy. But I am afraid that they might get thrown under the bus again as they have in the past.

What is the policy towards the Kurds and the fact that oftentimes they get left in the dust real quickly?

Ms. SLOTKIN. Well, again, I think the Kurds now more than ever are integrated into the State of Iraq. And while I think given their history there will always be concerns about them being quote ''left in the dust'' as you say, they are a part of the senior leadership of the government. They have come to some important agreements with the central government.

Mr. COOK. Okay. And their relationship with Turkey has obviously improved since we had the terrorists——

Ms. SLOTKIN. Significantly. I mean, if you would have told me as an Iraq expert a decade ago that they would have had the relations that they have with Turkey, I would have frankly laughed. I mean it is pretty——

Mr. COOK. I agree 100 percent.

Moving on real quick, a couple of Gulf States that I have real problems with and I won't mention, in terms of money going to Al Qaeda, and it is kind of wink-wink, nod-nod, or there has been reports of that, and these states are in our military—you know, it is as if they get a free ride on that. Is that true? And I am talking about one in particular and you might——

Ambassador PATTERSON. Well, no, sir, it is not true. There have been huge efforts over the years by our Treasury Department and others——

Mr. COOK. Maybe with the government, but they allow certain elements—I have got to move quickly, I am sorry.

Ambassador PATTERSON. Let me be quick. They don't allow it. They do try to shut it down. We try and shut it down.

Mr. COOK. But are there are citizens in that country that do funnel money to Al Qaeda?

Ambassador PATTERSON. They manage to fund these groups in places like Pakistan and Syria, of course. They are trying to restrain it, but, of course, it hasn't been 100 percent.

Mr. COOK. Okay. Going back to—I just want to make a real quick comment in regards to Iran. I am sorry, and I appreciate your service and everything and the Intel Community. Hey, I am a grunt, infantry. You know, you never, ever, ever, trust the intel because it is the grunts, my Marines that had to go in there and get the job done. And what happens? You get killed. And the best example going back was the Marine barracks in Lebanon.

And remember that group, Hezbollah, and who were they associated with? Iran. You talk to most of the military, at least the ones, the one country that keeps them awake at night is Iran, Iran, Iran. And to say we got a year, I don't believe it.

So, at least from one Congressman, I don't share that optimism. I have been to Israel. They are scared to death of what is happening there and it will be too late. And you are right, I don't think we can stop it unless we do have a good line in the sand that we are going to enforce.

I yield back. Thank you.

The CHAIRMAN. Thank you.

Mr. Smith.

Mr. SMITH. If I could follow up, this has been explored a great deal. I just want to follow up on a couple points about Iran and what we do about them. I mean, if our position is we just can't know, no matter what we do, we can't know, you know I guess isn't the only policy choice at that point to just declare war and get it over with? I mean, I am just not understanding where it is that the folks on this side of the aisle think that we ought to go with this.

Now, I will for a brief moment explain where it is that we are going with this that makes sense, and that is the sanctions were brought about to force Iran to the conclusion that building a nuclear weapon was not in their best interests.

In fact, you make a pretty powerful argument that the worst thing that Iran has done over the course of the last decade is pursue a nuclear weapon, because they were up to all manner of different malfeasance short of nuclear weapon, but some of that was tough to establish, it was tough to get our allies on board. But when they started pursuing a nuclear weapon our allies understood, gosh, even Russia understood, this was not a very good thing, so we were able to put crippling and crushing sanctions on them in a bipartisan way that brought Iran to the conclusion that they better talk.

And all of our intel shows us that they have not made the decision to build a nuclear weapon. In fact, someone said to me, well there is no evidence that that is true. I said I first heard that Iran was 6 months from getting a nuclear weapon in 2005. So what evidence is there that they have not decided to build one? They don't have one, all right? They were 6 months from it in 2005. If they wanted it, they would have it. They have not decided to build that weapon because they are not sure it is in their best interest to do so. So our policy is to keep the crippling sanctions on them.

And one of the things that was said that just really disturbed me was the notion that Iran is open for business as a result of this 6-month deal. Pay some attention to what is actually in the deal. All that is in there in terms of sanctions relief is to release a small amount of Iranian money that we have been holding. We are holding well over $100 billion, and I believe we are releasing somewhere between 4 and 6 billion. All of the other sanctions on their oil industry, on their financial services industry, all of those other sanctions are kept in place and are not going to be removed until we get a final agreement.

So if our position is, oh, goodness gracious, we can't possibly know, they might build it we can't trust them, then have the guts to say not just that we should have the option on the table, but that you are in favor of us bombing Iran right now today because we can't know.

I think that is wrong. I think it is a crazy policy, it is the wrong way to go, because we do know a great deal about what they are up to. The sanctions policy is our best hope to prevent them from getting a nuclear weapon. So these questions are pushing us in a direction that makes no logical sense. That is more of a statement than a question, obviously.

But help me out here, Ms. Slotkin. Is that not fairly accurate? And also it is clear, our policy is if everything else fails, we will use military force, but given the consequences of that we would dearly love to stop everything else from failing. So lay that out a little bit more clearly for us, because I think there is a clear policy here this committee is missing.

Ms. SLOTKIN. Thank you, sir. I think that is accurate. That is certainly the way we see it. I mean I think it is not crazy to have questions of trust with the Iranians.

Mr. SMITH. Sure.

Ms. SLOTKIN. That is a natural normal reaction to events that happened, God, for the past 30 years, with today being the anniversary, frankly.

Mr. SMITH. I think, if I may, our policy reflects that lack of trust.

Ms. SLOTKIN. Exactly. And I think that is why the interim agreement that is on the table right now is not about trust and just taking them at their word, it is about verification.

And my only point is if we were able to do it with the Soviet Union, right, if we were able to negotiate with others in our past who had every reason not to trust, with the right verification standards in place, I think we are able to make progress and we need to allow diplomacy a chance to succeed. Certainly from the Defense Department's perspective, I would always rather have diplomacy be the order of the day than be forced to take military action.

Mr. SMITH. Thank you.

The CHAIRMAN. I don't know that I would use Russia as an example of negotiating because we know that they have broken treaties.

And I think probably one of the things that leads us to the lack of trust is why do they have to do this work under a mountain? Why don't they just open it up? If they are just doing nuclear energy for energy, why do they have to bury it where it is away from sight? Where is the transparency?

Mr. SMITH. Again, Mr. Chairman——

Ms. SLOTKIN. Mr. Chairman——

The CHAIRMAN. We know that there are over 10 nations that use nuclear power but don't do the enriching that they are doing. So you know, there are some very solid reasons for distrusting them.

Mr. SMITH. Mr. Chairman, as I said, the cornerstone of our policy is we don't trust them, okay? We are not arguing—nobody is arguing in terms of how we negotiate this deal that we ought to just close our eyes and trust them. That is why we have the sanctions. That is why we have the back and forth.

Yes, absolutely Iran has been underhanded in this. What they want, they want to be able to build a bomb without having international repercussions. That is what they want. And they have been sort of dancing around for a decade trying to figure out how to do that, and it has been our job and the international community's job to say you can't. You know, if you go down this road the price you will pay will be steep. So, no, we don't trust them at all and we shouldn't.

The CHAIRMAN. And I think where we recently with this interim deal where we have the problem is the things I mentioned, and the thing that we put the sanctions on that brought them to the table, if we had kept those sanctions a little bit longer we may have gotten them to give up the enrichment, if that was what we really wanted.

Mr. SMITH. We haven't given up the sanctions. That is the whole point. What do you mean if we kept them a little longer? We have not given them up.

The CHAIRMAN. Yes, we did. You just said we gave them up $4 billion to $6 billion. In other words——

Mr. SMITH. And a whole raft of other sanctions are very firmly in place that are continuing to cripple their economy.

Let's ask Ms. Slotkin for her opinion. Is their economy any less crippled because we released a small amount of money?

Ambassador PATTERSON. No. Let me try—Mr. Chairman, one element that I think, it is not just our intelligence we are depending on, although I think it is pretty good in this instance. It is also the enhanced inspections by the IAEA that were a critical element of this interim agreement. They are going to be in some of these facilities every single day and others on a much more regular basis.

The CHAIRMAN. Okay. You know, this is already done and we are not going to undo it. We have had the same briefings and we just look at it a little bit differently, and I don't think it is because, Democrat or Republican.

Ms. SLOTKIN. Can I just add one—I am sorry, sir.

The CHAIRMAN. No.

Ms. SLOTKIN. Okay.

The CHAIRMAN. Let me get to the members who have been sitting here very patiently to ask their questions.

Dr. Wenstrup.

Dr. WENSTRUP. Thank you, Mr. Chairman. I appreciate you all being here today. If I can, we will go back to Iraq for a second.

You know, I think obviously the people of Fallujah and Anbar Province are not happy to see Al Qaeda back in Iraq, and you made some mention, Ms. Slotkin, that Al Qaeda probably would have resurged there in some way with or without our presence.

Ms. SLOTKIN. My point was Al Qaeda frankly was at its strongest right as we had the largest single number of troops in the country at a time, so 170,000 troops back in you know 2007 and we have got the highest rate of attack that we saw from Al Qaeda during the course of the war.

Dr. WENSTRUP. And I can appreciate that. I was there 2005 to 2006 you know leading up to that buildup and understand the effort that that takes. But I am just concerned that you may feel, and correct me if I am wrong, that a U.S. presence would have no deterrence.

Ms. SLOTKIN. I think the presence we were always talking about would be a train-advise presence, largely based out of Baghdad, right. The numbers we were talking about at the time were something around 10,000. So that is obviously not going to be able to have a geographic spread the way 170,000 troops had at the height of the surge. So I think while we would have been able to advise and assist in probably a more robust way, we had already turned over lead to the operations to the Iraqis a year and a half, 2 years before then.

So I don't think that we—our presence would have been the deterrent. I think we would have been able to provide more expertise and more training than we are currently doing.

Dr. WENSTRUP. You know, I tend to think our presence can be a deterrent. When I traveled to the Kurdish area, for example, they were pretty pleased there has been an American presence in their area since 1991, and I think that they probably, correct me if I am wrong, I don't know what kind of say they had at the table during the discussions on the SOFA, but I think they would have been more than happy to have an American presence in the Kurdish region of Iraq.

Did they have a say at the table during this conversation? I agree with what Mr. Courtney was bringing up about, you know, concern for our troops and protection for our troops. I understand that part completely. But I find it hard to believe that they would not have wanted our presence there.

Ms. SLOTKIN. Certainly different groups, and Iraq is made up of a large number of different groups, had different views on whether there should be a presence, a follow-on presence after 2011. There were Kurdish members of the original SOFA negotiating party. There were Kurdish members of parliament that voted on the SOFA when it passed back in 2008. And I think largely the Kurdish population tends to be pretty pro-American and would have supported us staying.

I don't think that speaks for everyone in the Kurdish territories, but I think there are also plenty of groups around the country, Shia, Sunni, and others who were supportive. They voted to keep us there. So the Kurds certainly weren't the only ones at the time who supported it.

Dr. WENSTRUP. With what is going on now, do you think they have any regrets?

Ms. SLOTKIN. I think you know, as we were talking about, if you go to Erbil, I am not sure where you were in the Kurdish areas, if go there, there are just cranes everywhere. They are——

Dr. WENSTRUP. I was at Sulaymaniyah.

Ms. SLOTKIN. Okay. So construction boomed, their economy is doing exceptionally well, they are signing important deals with their neighbors. They still have a senior role in the government. So I think that the Kurdish areas are doing particularly well and I think that is without us signing a follow-on agreement in 2011.

Dr. WENSTRUP. Admiral, I have a question. Strategically, what benefit do you think it would have had if we had a stronger presence in Iraq at this time? For the entire region, not just for Iraq?

Admiral PANDOLFE. Well, I don't want to speculate on what might have happened in Iraq. What I would like to focus on is Afghanistan and that we have, as Ms. Slotkin has underlined and Ambassador Patterson, we believe that the signing of a BSA [bilateral security agreement] there which reflects the will of their people and the international community, quite frankly, will allow us to maintain the presence, when I say ''we'' I mean the NATO presence, to help that nation continue toward a better future.

So looking forward it is our hope that Afghanistan, the president of Afghanistan does sign the BSA to allow the international community to remain in that country, both for defense purposes and to Ambassador Patterson's point for developmental purposes, because the international community presence will facilitate the flow of funds for both defense and for development.

The CHAIRMAN. Thank you.

Mr. Nugent.

Mr. NUGENT. Thank you, Mr. Chairman, and I want to thank this panel for being here.

I also really did enjoy the conversation between our ranking member and the chairman. I kind of liked that free-flowing dialogue. It is good.

You know I hear a lot about obviously trust as it relates to Iran. I was in Iraq in 2011 and had two sons in combat in Iraq in 2011 as they were transitioning out and I do remember that one night I was there an IRAM [improvised rocket-assisted missile] attack took place and killed a number of our troops. For those who don't know what an IRAM is, that is an Iranian warhead. The only place you can get an Iranian warhead is from Iran. And I worry about where we are in Afghanistan now just because Iran likes to play everywhere, and we see that across the board.

I think what a lot of folks are worried about, and particularly with Iran, you hear all kinds of estimates, so I get all the briefings, I sit on the IETC [Subcommittee on Intelligence, Emerging Threats and Capabilities], is the fact that once if they are successful in obtaining a nuclear weapon, we are going to be in the same position that we are today with North Korea. There are a whole lot of reasons how they got it, and we are going to be facing the same dilemma that we have today in North Korea but you know with a different state actor. And I guess that is why a number of us are concerned that we are going to make the same mistakes in this particular issue with Iran and particularly with our good friend and ally, with Israel, that could face the brunt of it.

I just don't know. We hear about sanctions. I heard the ranking member talk about sanctions. You know the Senate was just talking about increasing sanctions on Iran and I think they have paused that because of a lot of lobbying by the President in regards to not doing that. But why do you think that they were so, on both sides of the aisle in a bipartisan way, why do you think that they wanted to increase sanctions on Iran if they think that this is the right direction where we are going today with Iran in regards to them saying that they really don't want a nuclear weapon? Why do you think the Senate was taking that position? Do you have any idea? I am sure it is not just to block or, you know, cause problems for the President, because it was the Democrats who were pushing that.

Ambassador PATTERSON. Well, no, sir. I mean, I think as we have said, there is an enormous suspicion based on years of empirical data about Iran's intention. But let me stress that this nuclear—that Iran's ability to acquire a nuclear weapon is an existential threat to us and it is an existential threat to critically Iran's neighbors. So that has got to be our first priority.

And these sanctions, these crippling sanctions, the reduction of their capacity, their currency totally tanked, has enabled us to get to the table and try to negotiate this and to cap and to freeze their paths to a nuclear weapon while these negotiations are underway.

Mr. NUGENT. I mean, they are in control of this. I mean they could easily reverse this in regards to sanctions if they did what? What could they do today to reverse that? Is there something they could do today to reverse those sanctions?

Ambassador PATTERSON. Well, yes, because they could negotiate an agreement. There is an interim agreement and we have begun to negotiate. They could—there is, yes, a whole——

Mr. NUGENT. Couldn't they just walk away from what they are doing and still do the development they wanted to from a peaceful side, but could they not reverse this very simply if they wanted to, if they really didn't have a goal of creating a nuclear weapon?

Ambassador PATTERSON. Well, if they walked away from the negotiations? I am not quite sure I follow you, sir.

Mr. NUGENT. No, what I am saying could they not get the international partners and the United States to reverse their decision on those crippling sanctions if they did one thing, and clearly did the things that would be required to walk away from a nuclear weapon? Because that is really the name, is the reason we have these sanctions.

Ambassador PATTERSON. Well, sure they can lift the sanctions if they move in that direction, and that is what this negotiation is all about. It is an international negotiation with a number of countries, and there is a lot of U.N. Security Council resolutions that are at play too. So yes, as the negotiations go on, of course we hope that they will walk away from it.

Mr. NUGENT. And I will be honest with you, I am the last one that would want to see military action because I happen to have three sons that currently serve, and they are the brunt of—when we sit here and talk about military action, there is really a human face behind that and I want to make sure that before we do something that we, you know, allow the sanctions to work, but also allow diplomacy to work.

But at the end of the day, the Iranians have control. They control their fate in regards to what they do and the course of action that they have taken and are taking. And so while I appreciate everything that you do, I think that until they decide that they want to get out from underneath these sanctions, it is going to continue, because they have underlying reasons to do that.

And with that, Mr. Chairman, I yield back. I appreciate your time.

The CHAIRMAN. The gentleman's time has expired. No other questions, this hearing will stand adjourned. Thank you very much for your presence here.

[Whereupon, at 11:58 a.m., the committee was adjourned.]

APPENDIX

February 11, 2014

PREPARED STATEMENTS SUBMITTED FOR THE RECORD

FEBRUARY 11, 2014

Opening Statement of Chairman Howard P. "Buck" McKeon
"United States Security Policy and Defense Posture in the Middle East"
February 11, 2014

Good morning ladies and gentlemen. The committee meets to receive testimony on United States security policy and defense posture in the Middle East. Our witnesses include Ambassador Anne Patterson, Ms. Elissa Slotkin, and Vice Admiral Frank Pandolfe. Thank you for joining us today.

The committee has conducted several classified briefings and open hearings with outside experts on this topic area. However, today is an opportunity to build upon that knowledge in an open forum with senior policy and military leaders in our government.

The Middle East is in the midst of a particularly tumultuous period. From the Arab Awakening, to the evolution of al-Qaeda, to the deadly conflict in Syria, to Iran's continued pursuit of nuclear weapons; we are witnessing a level of volatility in the Middle East that poses a serious threat to U.S. security and our interests in the region.

While our allies and partners seek strong U.S. leadership and engagement in the region, they instead see signs of disengagement. Our withdrawals from Iraq and Afghanistan, the Administration's rebalance to other regions, and its deal-making with Iran, help to shape this view. There is widespread uncertainty about U.S. commitment to the Middle East. As noted by former U.S. Ambassador to Iraq, James Jeffrey, in a recent op-ed: "…as…often happens in this region, the Administration is sounding an uncertain tone… The result has been an extraordinary collapse of U.S. credibility in the region despite many commendable administration steps."

These comments illustrate a lack of certainty about U.S. policy in the region. Equally important is our military posture in the region – how we combat evolving threats, deter Iran, degrade al Qaeda, and assure our allies and partners. We also must ensure our military posture and its associated capabilities are not traded for interim deals with regimes that have a history of non-compliance.

We look forward to your testimony on the Administration's policy and posture in the Middle East, and how they comprehensively support U.S. national security interests.

Statement of Ranking Member Adam Smith
"United States Security Policy and Defense Posture in the Middle East"
February 11, 2014

There is no question that the Middle East has changed substantially over the last decade, and many of these changes are deeply concerning. In light of these changes, the Administration's has largely responded well and with a near-constant engagement in the region, but many challenges remain. I hope our witnesses will take the opportunity today to publicly lay out our past commitment to the region and how that commitment will evolve in the future.

The United States and our allies face a number of challenges in the Middle East—the rise of al Qaeda affiliated groups, the Iranian nuclear program, the civil war in Syria and the spillover effects from refugees in the region, political transition in Egypt, increased instability in Iraq, and the ongoing conflicts in Yemen. All are daunting and will take commitment, time, and enhanced cooperation with our partners in the region. We should remember some the notable successes we've had over the past five years and the potential for future success—U.S. troops are no longer in a grinding conflict in Iraq. Osama bin Laden, the founder of al Qaeda, is dead. We have an interim deal with Iran on their nuclear program, and there is a real chance that this problem can be resolved peacefully. Syria has agreed to give up its chemical weapons, and Secretary Kerry is hard at work at finding some way of ending the intractable conflict between the Palestinians and the Israelis.

But while there are possibilities of successes, we cannot minimize the very real, very serious, and very difficult problems we face. We have done a great deal to help our close ally Jordan deal with the destabilizing burden of Syria refugees, but I think we need to be creative to think hard about how we can do more. Lebanon's internal stability is threatened by the same dynamic, plus the spillover from Syria of violent groups intent on continuing their war in Lebanon.

Our Gulf partners and allies, especially Saudi Arabia, United Arab Emirates, and Qatar have all publicly, and in some cases privately, expressed concern with our policies on Syria. They have also expressed concern that any potential deal with Iran about their nuclear program will mean a diminishment of the U.S. commitment to defend them against Iranian aggression expressed through other means. We maintain an immensely powerful military force in the Gulf region, and Secretary Hagel rightly reminded everyone of this in his recent speech at the Manama Dialogue. The challenge will be maintaining this presence. In Syria, I believe we need to reengage with our allies. We may disagree about the risks of arming the opposition, but I do believe we can all agree on the risks posed by the Islamic State of Iraq and al Sham (ISIS).

We can and must take cooperative measures to ensure that ISIS and other al Qaeda associates cannot establish safe havens in Syria. Similarly, we should work with the government of Iraq to ensure they have the military equipment and advice they need to help combat ISIS, while we push the Maliki government to engage with the Sunni opposition and accommodate them politically.

We are also going to have to have a serious discussion with the Egyptians and with our friends in the region about how we can help Egypt. The recent political turmoil in that country, the economic challenges, and the crackdown on political opposition groups, pose real risks on ongoing instability in Egypt and for the region.

Israel is our steadfast partner. While much of what I have discussed lays out the challenges we face, we cannot forget our closest allies in the region. The Obama Administration has forged the closest military ties with Israel that have ever existed between our two countries and I expect that pattern to continue. Congress and the Administration have worked hard to ensure Israel's continued Qualitative Military Edge, a commitment we must keep in the future.

Finally, I end on a note of caution. While we work on the many challenges in the Middle East, we must be mindful of the limitations we face. If nothing else, our experiences in Iraq and Afghanistan should have taught us that we cannot remake societies on our own, and that there are real limits on how much and how fast we can push allies and partners. We can make progress, but it won't be as fast or as complete as any of us will like. All of this argues for patience and dedication and cooperation with our allies and in our own government.

Again, I would like to thank our witnesses for appearing today and the chairman for holding this hearing.

Testimony for the Record
Ambassador Anne W Patterson
Assistant Secretary of State for Near Eastern Affairs
U.S. Department of State
Armed Services Committee
U.S. House of Representatives
February 11, 2014

Chairman McKeon, Ranking Member Smith, and Members of the Committee, I am honored to appear before you today to offer an overview of U.S. foreign policy in the Middle East region – and I look forward to answering your questions. [With your permission, I request that my full statement be submitted for the record]

Mr. Chairman, I am glad to appear before you here today with my colleagues Vice Admiral Pandolfe and Principal Deputy Assistant Secretary for Defense and International Security Affairs, Elissa Slotkin. Together with the intelligence community, the Department of State and the Department of Defense work closely together to protect our country from terrorist attacks and to promote American national security objectives in this region.

The region today is undergoing a massive and historic change – and the United States is deeply engaged. Although a generation of American political leaders from both political parties had been urging the region's people to seek a democratic transformation, we were impressed at the speed with which the desire for change we had observed in so many countries finally surfaced.

There are many difficult challenges underlying the instability in the region today. It is a region where as many as 60 percent of the people are under age 30 – and where nearly a quarter of those people are unemployed. These young people are empowered by new communications technologies to see events across the world and to communicate with each other as never before. They are angered by rigid and corrupt governments that frustrate their desire for change, yet they have no experience with pluralist governance. And they are frustrated by national economies that are lagging – providing few jobs and little economic opportunity.

This broad discontent feeds instability and helps set the conditions for extremism. Our concern for peace and stability in the region requires that the United States remain firmly engaged. Our national security requires it; our ability to promote important values, such as universal rights, the rights of women, and religious freedoms require it; and our and the region's aspirations for broader trade and investment in what could be a surging regional economy requires it.

Mr. Chairman, in this very complex region, our best chance to resolve some of the world's most difficult foreign policy challenges and to do so without having to resort to force, requires vigorous diplomacy. With your support, our people will continue our engagement in the Middle East, knowing that there is no absolute guarantee of safety, to protect our country and pursue the national security interests of the United States.

Secretary of State John Kerry has underscored our belief that America's global leadership can be demonstrated through diplomatic efforts – and he has taken extraordinary personal efforts to address the region's most pressing challenges: preventing Iran from obtaining a nuclear weapon, ending the civil war in Syria, and reaching a final status agreement between the Israelis and Palestinians.

It is in our interest to use diplomacy and engagement in order to resolve conflict and build the capacity of our partners, which is exactly what we are doing. With elections coming up in key countries this spring – Iraq, Egypt, and others – supporting inclusive, free, fair and open political processes transitioning towards democracy is critical to bolstering moderate political actors and isolating extremists in the region.

Iran
I know this committee shares our deep concern about Iran's nuclear program and its intentions. I want to reassure you that the United States government is firmly committed to preventing Iran from acquiring a nuclear weapon. On January 20, we and our P5+1 partners, and the European Union, began to implement the Joint Plan of Action with Iran. For the first time in nearly a decade, Iran has agreed to halt progress on its nuclear program and roll it back in key respects.

Secretary Kerry met with Iranian Foreign Minister Mohammad Javad Zarif at the recent Munich security conference, where he reiterated the importance of both sides negotiating in good faith and called on Iran to abide by its commitments under the Joint Plan of Action. He also reaffirmed that if Iran does not keep its commitments during this period, we will halt the limited, temporary and reversible relief envisioned in the Joint Plan of Action.

We are now focused on pursuing a comprehensive solution – discussions will begin in Vienna on February 18. We plan to build our initial steps to obtain verifiable assurances that Iran's nuclear program is peaceful and that Iran will not acquire a nuclear weapon. During this period, we will continue to enforce vigorously the existing sanctions put in place by the United States and many of our partners in the international community.

We are well aware that Iran continues to promote regional instability and uses both Iranian and proxy fighters to pursue foreign policy objectives. Iranian money, training, and equipment are playing a significant role in keeping the Asad regime in power, exacerbating a conflict that has wide-reaching regional security implications. And of course, Iran's support for Hezbollah in Lebanon has done much to destabilize the country and assure tensions continue along its U.N.-recognized border with Israel. Iran's efforts to undermine Yemen's stability and peaceful political transition were revealed when Yemeni forces intercepted a shipment of Iranian weapons being smuggled into Yemen last year. Iran has provided aid to extremist elements seeking to undermine Bahrain's stability and security. Our efforts to reach a diplomatic solution to the nuclear issue will not stop us from taking decisive steps with our partners to prevent this interference.

The U.S. government continues to be concerned about the Iranian government's violations of its own citizens' human rights. We will continue to advocate for greater Iranian government accountability in international fora and imposing sanctions on Iranian officials and institutions that violate Iranians' human rights.

Iraq

Iraq has, regrettably, been experiencing escalating levels of violence. The two-way flow of Sunni extremists between Syria and Iraq has had a direct bearing on high-profile attacks in Iraq. In 2011 and 2012, about 4,400 Iraqis civilians and members of the security forces were killed each year – many in attacks led by Islamic State of Iraq and the Levant (ISIL), formerly known as al-Qaeda in Iraq.

Last year, ISIL began shifting resources from Syria to Iraq in search of new opportunities consistent with their broader ambitions. By the summer of 2013, the number of suicide attacks in Iraq had climbed from an average of 5-10 per month to approximately 30-40 per month. These attacks were calculated, coordinated and unfortunately, increasingly effective and were directed not only at Shia civilian targets but also Sunni and Kurdish targets. On January 1, ISIL launched its most brazen attack yet, and occupied portions of the Anbar cities of Ramadi and Fallujah. The Iraqi government, working together with local leaders in Anbar and with important U.S. support has pushed back; Ramadi now faces isolated pockets of resistance from anti-government fighters, and the government hopes to clear terrorists from Fallujah predominately by using local tribal forces. But this violence has had a devastating effect on the people of Iraq. The United Nations reports at least 8,800 civilians and members of the security forces were killed in violent attacks across Iraq in 2013. The need for political leaders to overcome mistrust and reach compromises on essential political reforms is urgent.

We continue to press upon Iraq's government the importance of working with local Sunni leaders to draw the nation together in the fight against ISIL. The United States will continue to support the people of Iraq and their government to secure the city of Fallujah.

We also continue to work closely with Iraq's leaders to help them build a long-term political, economic and security strategy and to support the national election scheduled for April 30, 2014. I would like to thank the Congress for its support for the much-needed military equipment we have been able to provide to Iraq. To combat the very real extremist threats, Iraq needs a professional and well-equipped army that can provide the capability for the government to engage extremist groups proactively long before they enter the cities.

Syria
We have a team on the ground in Geneva, working with U.N. Joint Special Representative for Syria Lakhdar Brahimi, our London 11 partners and the Syrian opposition as it sits across the table from the Syrian regime for a second round of negotiations. Their goal is to push for traction on discussions regarding a transition process and confidence building measures. A primary focus for the United States during this round will be to ensure humanitarian access to civilians in Syria caught in the middle of the conflict.

The scope of the catastrophe in Syria is enormous – it is estimated that more than 136,000 people have been killed; more than 2.4 million people affected by the conflict have fled to neighboring countries while, inside Syria, an additional 6.5 million people are internally displaced and 9.3 million people are in desperate need of humanitarian assistance. The United States has responded to this crisis by providing more than $1.7 billion in humanitarian assistance, the largest of any nation. These resources support international and non-governmental organizations assisting those affected by the conflict inside Syria and across the region.

Outrageously, the Syrian regime has responded to international humanitarian efforts with an apparent policy to obstruct or delay access at every point, denying aid to more than 250,000 civilians trapped in besieged areas, including cities in East Ghouta and the city of Mouadhamiyah as well as Homs.

For nearly three years, the Syrian regime has chosen to tighten its grip on power, tar all opposition as "terrorists" and plunge Syria into civil war, rather than accede to the will and aspiration of its people.

As the fighting has dragged on, the conflict has attracted extremists seeking to take advantage of the loss of state authority. This includes terrorist groups, such as the Nusrah Front and Islamic State of Iraq and the Levant (ISIL), that openly compete for territory with the moderate Syrian opposition, with the regime and, until recently, with each other. ISIL has used its foothold in Syria as a base for expanded attacks in Iraq. The extremists have played directly into the hands of the Asad regime by attempting to force the Syrian people and the world into a false choice between Asad's continued oppression or a new form of oppression under extremists.

The expanded presence of these extremist elements in Syria has weakened the ability of Syria's moderate opposition to unite Syrians behind its leadership in the civil war. We see no military solution for this terrible conflict – only greater humanitarian suffering and growing extremist participation as the conflict continues. Instead, the United States has worked to build international consensus for bringing this conflict to a close.

Although the Geneva II process has begun, we all know that this is just the beginning. The support demonstrated by the United Nations and over 40 countries and organizations for a peaceful, stable, inclusive Syria will be crucial as we move forward. We will continue to play a vigorous role in the difficult work of helping the parties move forward.

President Obama and Secretary Kerry have denounced the use of chemical weapons by the Syrian regime in this conflict. We are working closely with the Organization for the Prohibition of Chemical Weapons (OPCW) and a number of international partners, as the UN-OPCW's Joint Mission works to meet the ambitious June 30 target date for the total elimination of Syria's chemical weapons program. All of its chemical weapons production and mixing equipment has been destroyed. We are currently working with the OPCW to destroy Syria's remaining chemical weapons and precursors, but Syria has slowed delivery of these materials to the port of Latakia for removal and destruction, citing safety, logistical, and security concerns. We are concerned about the slow pace adopted by the government of Syria, and the impact this is having on the overall chemical weapons elimination effort. The United States, along with the international community, is very closely monitoring the implementation of UNSCR 2118, and we are taking appropriate steps to urge Syria to fulfill all of its obligations.

Lebanon

The people of Lebanon have been struggling to build an independent, stable government for generations. They were frustrated for many years by the Syrian military presence, and they continue to suffer at the hands of Hezbollah, armed and supported by Iran and Syria.

The Lebanese people deserve a government that responds to their needs and protects their interests. Any new government must address Lebanon's urgent security and political problems: responding to the needs of Lebanese communities hosting nearly one million refugees from Syria; strengthening national institutions; countering extremist ideologies and redoubling counterterrorism efforts; encouraging offshore energy development; and ensuring that the business of the government – including presidential and parliamentary elections – is conducted in a timely, transparent, and fair manner.

The United States will continue to support the Lebanese Armed Forces and other state security institutions to protect Lebanese sovereignty and to provide stability and security for Lebanon. Over the past year alone, the United States is providing $71.2 million in FY 2013 Foreign Military Financing to the LAF.

Jordan

We maintain a strong partnership with Jordan, a key partner on Middle East Peace, and President Obama is looking forward to meeting King Abdullah later this week. Jordan has been a strong and consistent partner in Middle East peacemaking and a bulwark against extremism in the region. We are committed to supporting Jordan in its efforts to secure its borders and prevent any spillover of fighting from Syria.

Jordan faces tremendous challenges coping with the influx of almost 600,000 refugees from the continuing civil war in Syria. To help Jordan manage the growing burden on its communities, infrastructure and public services, we have provided more than $268 million in humanitarian assistance for programs to help address the needs of refugees and the communities in Jordan that host them.

We have supported Jordan's economic and political stability through five-year assistance Memorandum of Understanding, which provides annually $360 million in Economic Support Funds and $300 million in Foreign Military Financing. To help Jordan mitigate the costs of hosting almost 600,000 Syrian refugees and external shocks resulting from the regional unrest, we have provided significant additional assistance in FY 2012 and FY 2013, including $300 million in cash transfers and a $1.25 billion loan guarantee to facilitate Jordan's access to less costly international financing. Our partnership includes the achievement of important milestones, including the establishment of a bilateral free trade agreement with Jordan, which has opened U.S. markets up to Jordanian products, and we intend to work closely with the Jordanians to support the modernization of their economy.

Israel, the Palestinians and Middle East Peace
The United States and Israel share a deep bond and close ties. Our foreign policy is rooted in the strong support of the American people for Israel's right to live in peace within secure and defensible borders. Under President Obama, the security relationship between our countries has never been stronger. We have more military, intelligence, and diplomatic exchanges with Israel than ever before. The United States is committed to ensuring that Israel maintains its qualitative military edge so it can counter and defeat any credible threat from any state, coalition, or non-state actor.

The Palestinian people also deserve to live within secure and defined borders. Like people everywhere, Palestinians seek to build their nation and better lives for themselves and their children. We continue to provide assistance to the Palestinian Authority's Security Forces to enhance stability and combat terrorism in support of our efforts to achieve a two-state solution.

Over the past year, the United States has committed a tremendous amount of effort to working with Israelis and Palestinians toward reaching a final status peace agreement. The goal is to support the parties as they reach for an agreement that would end the conflict and address all the core issues.

Security has been a critical focus thus far, and we have put the full range of resources of the U.S. Government behind this effort in an unprecedented way. For the past nine months, a team led by General John Allen has been engaged in a comprehensive security dialogue with our Israeli and Palestinian counterparts.

In the end, this agreement must be accepted and embraced by the parties. The United States continues to oppose attempts to impose solutions in international fora and efforts to delegitimize the State of Israel. We oppose efforts to impose economic, political or academic sanctions or boycotts against Israel – a clear and longstanding policy reinforced by Secretary Kerry.

Peace can bring enormous benefits to both sides. Palestinians stand to gain, above all else, an independent, viable, contiguous state, their own place among the community of nations. And for Israel, the benefits of peace are enormous as well, perhaps even more significant. No nation on earth stands to gain so many new economic partners so quickly as Israel does, because 20 additional members – nations of the Arab League and 35 Muslim countries stand ready under the Arab Peace Initiative to recognize Israel and normalize relations the moment a peace agreement is reached. Together, the Jewish state of Israel and the Arab state of Palestine can develop into an international hub for technology, for trade, and tourism that could invigorate the entire region.

Egypt

The situation in Egypt, the largest Arab country, is deeply worrisome. Egypt has been a close strategic partner for decades. We continue to support the Egyptian people's aspiration to establish a democratic government that respects universal rights, helps address their economic challenges, and promotes employment and investment opportunities.

In the months ahead, the Egyptian people will have an opportunity to choose a new President and parliament, as set forth in the interim government's roadmap. While the constitutional referendum in January was an important step in Egypt's transition, it did not bring any resolution to Egypt's very deep political polarization. We hope that the upcoming elections will produce a government that is respected and broadly accepted by the Egyptian people – and that improves the stability and economic prospects of the country.

We now look to the Egyptian government to implement the rights guaranteed under Egypt's new constitution. We have strong concerns with regard to the actions they have taken to limit dissent, curtail freedom of expression -- including for members of the press-- freedom of peaceful assembly, and to stifle political and civil society opposition.

At the same time, we remain concerned about the serious security threats that Egypt faces. Drawn by the political unrest in Egypt over the past two years and seeking new opportunities, extremist groups continue to conduct violent attacks against the Egyptian government and attempt to launch attacks from Egyptian territory against Israel.

We appreciate Congress' willingness to work with us to continue our assistance to Egypt. Thanks to your support, we have the necessary flexibility to further our strategic interests in Egypt and the region as events unfold. We are working with other donors to Egypt – particularly those in the Gulf – to coordinate future assistance to the Egyptian government in a manner that more effectively encourages credible and sustainable reforms of Egypt's economy.

Gulf Security

As you know, the White House has announced that President Obama will travel to Saudi Arabia next month to personally engage King Abdullah and the Saudi leadership and move forward our important dialogue on regional security matters.

Our friends in the Gulf have not been immune from some of the economic challenges and social unrest that have affected other countries in the region. They are also deeply concerned about security matters in their very important and economically sensitive neighborhood.

We remain committed to the security of the Gulf region and have enjoyed strong cooperation with our Gulf Cooperation Council (GCC) partners on regional foreign policy and security issues while maintaining a sizeable security presence in the region. Through the U.S.-GCC Strategic Cooperation Forum, we have enhanced our cooperation on regional security matters and seen real advances in cooperation on issues including ballistic missile defense. This strong relationship allows us to work closely with our Gulf allies to address issues of mutual concern. They have been deeply supportive of the Secretary's efforts to achieve Middle East Peace and of efforts to bring stability to Lebanon.

Our strong relationships also allow us to have frank conversations about areas where our approaches may differ, permitting us to work together and develop solutions to regional problems. Secretary Kerry and other senior U.S. officials will continue our discussions with our friends in the Gulf in the lead up to the President's upcoming trip to Saudi Arabia.

Yemen

Yemen's President Abdo Rabbo Mansour Hadi and the Yemeni people recently concluded the country's historic National Dialogue, a critical milestone in the implementation of the GCC initiative, which guides Yemen's peaceful political transition. We, in partnership with the international community, are encouraging and supporting Yemen in implementing the recommendations of the Dialogue and subsequent stages in the nation's transition and stand ready to assist them.

While Yemen continues to make significant progress in its path to democracy, it faces unprecedented challenges, including a dire economic situation, and violence instigated by one of the most potent Al-Qaeda affiliates in the world. With our partners in the region, we must continue to find ways to promote economic growth, including job creation and development of private enterprise, and necessary reform. Continued international support for Yemen's transition is critical as the Yemeni people create a more democratic and stable country that can meet the needs of its citizens and contribute to regional security.

Libya

The United States supports the Libyan people in their search for a stable, democratic and prosperous future after 42 years of authoritarian misrule – and since the Libyan revolution in 2011 we have been working closely with the new Libyan government.

Libya has the potential to be a strong partner, but its governmental structures are weak. The country also faces serious security and political challenges as it works to fulfill the peaceful and democratic aspirations of its revolution.

The United States has two strategic goals in Libya: supporting the development of a basic security capability in the face of domestic and regional threats and progress on Libya's democratic transition, including the establishment of a functioning national government. By fostering increased security and better governance, we also help to facilitate greater private sector engagement in Libya to begin to diversify the economy and generate jobs for Libya's youth.

At the request of the Libyan government, our recent efforts have focused on improving Libya's security. Our Defense Department colleagues plan to train 5,000-8,000 general purpose forces (GPF) as part of a larger effort with the UK, Italy, Turkey and Bulgaria over the next few years to improve security in Libya, an important step in facilitating Libya's transition. As part of this program, funded by the Libyan government, we will also conduct an unprecedented vetting and screening of trainees that participate in the program.

Looking forward, we also plan to increase focus on helping Libya's institutions govern effectively, meet the needs of the Libyan people, and advance the democratic transition.

Maghreb-Sahel Security

Instability in the region, porous borders, and the collapse of state institutions in northern Mali have increased regional threats and created new opportunities for cross border illicit flows and for violent extremist groups, such as al-Qaeda in the Maghreb (AQIM), to gain ground and stage operations in both the Maghreb and the Sahel. We have established an interagency Sahel-Maghreb Working Group to address the cross-regional and multi-dimensional nature of these threats. We are also encouraging bilateral and regional partnerships among key countries by building on platforms, such as the Trans-Sahara Counterterrorism Partnership (TSCTP) and the Global Counterterrorism Forum (GCTF), in order to respond to violent extremism, improve border security, and build CT capacity in the region.

Tunisia

Tunisia remains one of the region's best hopes for a successful transition to democracy. Three years after the start of the Arab Awakening, the promise of dignity, democracy, and a better future in Tunisia took tremendous steps forward in January. Demonstrating leadership and pragmatism, political leaders in Tunisia undertook important compromises and adopted a new constitution and formed an independent interim government that will steer the country to parliamentary and presidential elections for a permanent government.

President Obama called Prime Minister Mehdi Jomaa last week to congratulate him and the Tunisian people and to promise America's continued partnership as they complete Tunisia's transition to democracy. He invited the Prime Minister to visit Washington later this year.

Economic Issues and the Region's Future

As I mentioned at the outset, the region continues to face serious challenges to peace and stability. In many countries, some of the fundamentals of their economics present obstacles to the kind of economic growth that can buoy new governments and peoples' hopes for the future.

I have long felt that the United States needs to focus greater attention on the fundamentals of economic growth and trade policies in the region – beyond the traditional diplomatic challenges of managing relationships for peace and security. We need to help leaders focus on policies for jobs and growth that will benefit their people and knit their economies closer to the United States and the opportunities of the global economy. Secretary Kerry has an even more expansive view: he has appointed a special adviser with global responsibilities to bring focus to our

Department's engagement with economic and commercial affairs in a world where security, stability and prosperity are inextricably intertwined with economic power. The Secretary is calling upon all of our Embassies to show diplomatic leadership to advance U.S. economic and commercial interests as well as to support economic progress for people around the world.

So while working to resolve disputes that threaten the peace and security of this region, we are also looking at the ways in which governments and business can be partners in its economic growth and transformation. Progress in diplomatic agreements can help turn the extraordinary creativity and energy of people in this region toward the building of a better future – but it will take work, because the uphill climb from here is steep.

Conclusion
Mr. Chairman, Ranking Member Smith, members of the committee, I appreciate the opportunity to appear before you today and I look forward to answering any questions you may have.

Anne Woods Patterson: Assistant Secretary for Near Eastern Affairs

Anne Patterson is a Career Ambassador in the Foreign Service. She was Ambassador to Egypt from 2011-2013, Ambassador to Pakistan, 2007-2010, Ambassador to Colombia, 2000-2003, and Ambassador to El Salvador, 1997-2000. She has also served as Assistant Secretary of State for International Narcotics and Law Enforcement Affairs, Deputy Permanent Representative at the US Mission to the United Nations, and the Deputy Inspector General of the Department.

A forty-year veteran of the Foreign Service, Mrs. Patterson has served in a variety of economic and political positions in the Department of State and abroad. She is a two-time recipient of the Secretary's Distinguished Service Award and was named one of Foreign Policy's Top 100 Global Thinkers in 2011. A native of Fort Smith Arkansas, Mrs. Patterson graduated from Wellesley College and is married to retired Foreign Service Officer David Patterson. They have four children.

OPENING REMARKS OF
PRINCIPAL DEPUTY ASSISTANT SECRETARY OF DEFENSE
FOR INTERNATIONAL SECURITY AFFAIRS

BEFORE THE HOUSE ARMED SERVICES COMMITTEE ON

MIDDLE EAST REGIONAL POLICY AND BILATERAL AND
MULTILATERAL RELATIONSHIPS

FEBRUARY 11, 2014

Chairman McKeon, Ranking Member Smith and other distinguished members of the Committee, I appreciate the opportunity to speak to you about our multilateral and bilateral defense relationships in the Middle East and how these partnerships fit into our broader regional policy.

In broad terms, our strategy involves cooperating with regional partners and the international community in order to help foster a Middle East that is stable, peaceful and prosperous – and that, over time, succeeds in fulfilling the aspirations of its own people: for a greater say in their national affairs; for the broadening of human opportunity; and for the recognition of the rights and the dignity of every individual.

The continuing ripples of the Arab Spring and ongoing political transitions in many countries in the Middle East offer the United States both opportunities and challenges as we work to address core interests: combating Al-Qa'ida and affiliated movements; confronting external aggression directed at our allies and partners; ensuring the free flow of energy from the region to the rest of the world; and preventing the development, proliferation, and use of weapons of mass destruction.

In short, the greater Middle East remains a region of vital strategic importance to the United States. This is a point this Administration has made repeatedly – including in the 2012 Defense Strategic Guidance, which affirms that "the United States will continue to place a premium on U.S. and allied military presence in – and support of – partner nations in and around this region."

Even as we have undertaken drawdowns from Iraq and now Afghanistan, and initiated a rebalance toward the Asia-Pacific region, we have held strong to this commitment to our regional partners in the Middle East.

At the core of this commitment are critical tools that the Department of Defense uses to achieve U.S. goals in the region: our force posture; our bilateral partnerships; our growing multilateral relationships; and our military exercises across the region. I'll briefly talk about each of these in turn.

Force Posture

First, force posture. The most tangible sign of commitment we can make to the security of the region is the physical presence of our men and women in uniform, as well as the presence of our advanced military equipment.

Anyone – friend or foe – who looks at our presence in the Middle East will come to only one conclusion: our commitment to the Middle East is in no way eroding.

Let me give you just a few examples of that commitment.

- We have a ground, air, and naval presence of more than 35,000 U.S. forces in and around the immediate vicinity of the Gulf.

- We have deployed our most advanced fighter aircraft throughout the region, including F-22s, to ensure that we can quickly respond to contingencies.

- We have deployed our most advanced intelligence, surveillance, and reconnaissance (ISR) assets to provide a continuous picture of activities in and around the Gulf.

- We have fielded an array of missile defense capabilities, including ballistic missile defense ships, Patriot batteries, and sophisticated radars throughout the region.

- We routinely maintain a naval presence of more than 40 ships in the region, including a carrier strike group, and conduct a range of freedom of navigation operations. These operations have included approximately 50 transits of the Strait of Hormuz over the past six months.

Bilateral Partnerships

I will turn now to the second tool we are using to advance our security interests in the region: bilateral partnerships.

For several decades now, we have sought to advance our security interests by investing in close bilateral ties with vital partners. We are strengthening military-to-military relationships in the region, working to enable effective local capacity, and cooperating with international and regional partners as part of a coordinated interagency approach. These bilateral partnerships are the critical enablers for advancing our interests through sustained U.S. leadership.

We use a wide variety of security cooperation activities to interact with our partners in support of these efforts. These include: State-led and DoD-executed Foreign Military Sales (FMS) and Foreign Military Financing (FMF) programs; Building Partnership Capacity (BPC) programs; cooperative research and development and defense industrial cooperation; the State-DoD International Military Education and Training (IMET) programs; and other initiatives that build engagement with our partners, foster mutual understanding, and advance our regional objectives.

The Middle East is home to one of the most important bilateral security relationships we have anywhere in the world – and that, of course, is with Israel.

The U.S.-Israel Defense relationship remains stronger than ever. In addition to the FMF program, DoD contributes to Israeli security by maintaining Israel's Qualitative Military Edge (QME) and supporting the State Department's efforts to authorize the sale of advanced technology to Israel; conducting combined training and exercises for the defense of Israel; and supporting active missile defense efforts, to include funding for programs such as Iron Dome.

Israel faces turmoil and uncertainty from across the region. Yet, despite these immense challenges, the bond between the United States and Israel is unbreakable, and our defense relationship is stronger than ever. President Obama has been unequivocal in his commitment to Israel's security, and the Department of Defense is working tirelessly in support of that commitment.

This is not just rhetoric – it is backed by concrete actions. The United States is providing $3.1 billion dollars in FMF to Israel this year, as part of a 10-year $30 billion dollar commitment to Israel. The President has already pledged to begin negotiations on extending this security assistance even further into the future.

The Department of Defense also continues to work in conjunction with the Department of State to ensure that Israel maintains its Qualitative Military Edge. Israel must have the ability to defeat any regional threat. To maintain this edge, the United States continues to provide Israel with the most advanced technology available – including the F-35 and the V-22 Osprey.

DoD is also committed to its support for Israel's multi-layered Missile and Rocket Defense (Iron Dome). In Fiscal Year 2013 alone, DoD provided more than $440 million to Israel for its missile defense programs in addition to the $3.1 billion Israel receives in Foreign Military Financing. The outstanding performance of Iron Dome has had a crucial role in the recent operation Pillar of Defense.

Finally, DoD is actively working to support the ongoing Israel-Palestinian negotiations, and Secretary Kerry's diplomatic efforts. President Obama, Secretary of Defense Hagel, and Secretary of State Kerry designated General John Allen to play a key role in analyzing security challenges in the context of these negotiations. General Allen and his team of experts continue to meet with their Israeli and Palestinian counterparts to discuss concepts for potential security arrangements that will provide greater security for Israel and for a future independent and sovereign Palestinian state.

Another bilateral security relationship that is important to achieving U.S. goals in the region is our relationship with Egypt.

The U.S.-Egypt relationship is one of our most significant and enduring strategic defense relationships in the Middle East. For more than thirty years it has served to further our countries' joint security interests.

Egypt is an important regional actor and our security partnership with the Egyptians facilitates cooperation on counter-terrorism efforts, eases U.S. military access and critical over-flight privileges, helps improve the security of Israel, and contributes to the security of our embassy and consulate.

As the President and Secretary Hagel have made clear, we have serious concerns with the events of last July and August, and our hold on delivery of four large-scale weapon systems is a demonstration of that. The United States wants Egypt's transition to succeed, which will ensure our security relationship is maintained and our interests are protected over the long term. We continue to use our relationship with Egyptian military and civilian leaders to encourage an inclusive, non-violent transition that meets the aspirations of the Egyptian people.

Another important bilateral relationship we continue to work on is with the Government of Iraq. Since 2011, we have normalized our security cooperation with Iraq by forming the Office of Security Cooperation-Iraq (OSC-I), under the U.S. Embassy, and reducing its size from more than 700 uniformed U.S. military personnel performing Title 22 activities to 108 personnel today.

We have been tracking the uptick in violence and the situation in Anbar very closely. We, along with our State Department colleagues and others in the U.S. Government, have been urging the Government of Iraq that the only long-term way to defeat the Islamic State in Iraq and the Levant (ISIL) is through robust cooperation with Sunni leaders and we continue to encourage the Prime Minister to address Sunni grievances. Iraq will only be secure when all Iraqis are included in the political, economic, and social life of the country.

In addition, we have provided the Government of Iraq with expedited delivery of defense articles to resupply Iraqi Security Forces fighting terrorists in Anbar, assisted with additional tools so that the Iraqis can increase surveillance capabilities, and through OSC-

I, are conducting non-operational training of Defense Ministry leadership and the Iraqi Counter Terrorism Services.

Multilateral Relationships

As important as our bilateral relationships may be, our policy in the Middle East also depends on multilateral ties.

The complexities of competing interests, internal politics and diverse capabilities among our regional partners make multilateral efforts all the more difficult. However, we have had success in regional multilateral efforts to counter piracy, combat regional extremism, establish cooperative air and missile defense, and carry out operational exercises – and we believe there is more we can do.

One recent multilateral initiative was the President's determination that makes the Gulf Cooperation Council (GCC) eligible to be furnished with U.S. defense articles and services as a single entity. This designation will help us to work with Gulf Cooperation Council member states to enhance critical capabilities, including items for ballistic missile defense, maritime security, and counter-terrorism.

Building on the momentum of the U.S.-GCC Strategic Cooperation Forum chaired by Secretaries Kerry and Hagel this past September, we are currently working on a first-ever Defense Ministerial event with the GCC sometime this year.

Of course, multilateral relationships are especially important in contexts where our national security depends upon broad diplomatic support.

The United States continues to support United Nations (UN)-Arab League Joint Special Representative Brahimi and the Syrian opposition in their efforts to find a negotiated political solution to the Syrian crisis, and the creation of a transitional governing body within the framework of the June 2012 Geneva Communique.

We know this will be a long process and that it won't be easy, given the complexity of all the issues and the wide gaps that exist between the parties. We will continue to work with the UN, Russia, and the international community to do what we can to help move this process forward. We will also continue to closely watch the multilateral effort to ensure the destruction of Syria's chemical-weapons arsenal.

Another difficult regional situation that we have sought to address with multilateral engagement is the often-destabilizing behavior of the government of Iran.

Let me once again reiterate what this Administration has said repeatedly: we will not allow Iran to acquire a nuclear weapon. Our strategy of pressure and engagement – a strategy made possible by a strong, multilateral sanctions program – has created a window for diplomacy, and the Joint Plan of Action was an important first step. We are now focused on testing the prospects for a comprehensive nuclear deal based on verifiable actions that convince us – and the international community – that Iran is not trying to obtain a nuclear bomb.

The Department fully supports these diplomatic efforts, while continuing to focus intently on ensuring that the President has all options available should negotiations falter or Iran not abide by its commitments. This includes contingency planning and maintaining a capable military posture in the region that helps remind Iran that diplomacy is the preferred option of the United States, not the only option. We also remain cognizant of Iran's nefarious regional activities – such as its continued support of the Assad regime and terrorist groups like Lebanese Hezbollah – and we remain committed to addressing those challenges.

Military Exercises

Finally, the Department's military exercises help us advance security relationships in the Middle East – both bilateral and multilateral.

They include:

- Eagle Resolve, an annual multi-national naval, land, and air exercise designed to enhance regional cooperative defense efforts of the Gulf Cooperation Council (GCC) and U.S. Central Command. In 2013, this exercise included 12 nations, 2,000 soldiers, sailors, airmen, and Marines, and 1,000 counterpart personnel from GCC countries.

- Eager Lion, an annual exercise designed to strengthen tactical proficiency in critical mission areas, support long-term relationships, and enhance regional security and stability by responding to modern-day security scenarios. In 2013, the exercise involved 8,000 personnel from 19 nations including 5,000 U.S. personnel from across all Military Services.

- And finally, the Mine Countermeasures Exercise – in 2013, U.S. Naval Forces Central Command hosted the international Mine Countermeasures Exercise, which included 40 nations, 6,000 service members, and 35 ships across 8,000 nautical miles, stretching from the Gulf to the Strait of Hormuz.

These exercises help reinforce multilateral ties within the Middle East and with international partners around the globe.

Thank you, Members of the Committee, for this opportunity to discuss with you the primary tools we are using to advance our security priorities in a rapidly changing Middle East. I look forward to your questions.

Elissa Slotkin

**Performing the Duties of the Principal Deputy
Under Secretary of Defense for Policy**

Elissa Slotkin is currently the Principal Deputy Assistant Secretary of Defense for International Security Affairs, where she and the Assistant Secretary oversee policy development and implementation on the Middle East, Africa, Europa/NATO and Russia. She joined the Office of the Secretary of Defense for Policy in 2011 as the Senior Adviser for Middle East Transition, and prior to that served in the State Department where she worked closely with Secretary Clinton, then-Deputy Secretary Jack Lew, and later Deputy Secretary Tom Nides on Iraq policy during the transition from military to civilian lead. Elissa has also served on the National Security Council Staff as Director for Iraq, where her portfolio included a leading role in the drafting of the U.S-Iraq Status of Forces Agreement. Her career in government began in the intelligence community, where she served in Iraq for nearly 24 months total and as Special Assistant to the first Director of National Intelligence, John Negroponte. In addition to her government experience, Elissa has worked at non-profit organizations in the Middle East and East Africa. She received her undergraduate degree from Cornell and her Masters degree from Columbia's School of International and Public Affairs.

HOUSE ARMED SERVICES COMMITTEE

STATEMENT OF

VICE ADMIRAL FRANK C. PANDOLFE, USN

DIRECTOR OF STRATEGIC PLANS AND POLICY

JOINT CHIEFS OF STAFF

BEFORE THE HOUSE ARMED SERVICES COMMITTEE

MIDDLE EAST POLICY

11 FEBRUARY 2014

HOUSE ARMED SERVICES COMMITTEE

Chairman McKeon, Ranking Member Smith, and distinguished Committee Members, thank you for this opportunity to update you regarding how our military forces are supporting U.S. policy objectives in the Middle East.

Our interests in that vital and unsettled part of the world are significant, and we are committed to working with the states of the region to strengthen security, enhance deterrence, and prevent war.

The U.S. seeks to increase regional stability, decrease violent extremism, and counter the proliferation and use of Weapons of Mass Destruction against our nation, our allies, and our partners. We cannot do these things alone. Rather, to accomplish these goals, we work together every day with other agencies of our government, with forward stationed State Department professionals, and with partner countries in the region.

All these missions require us to maintain significant combat power forward and to continually interact with our partners by way of operations, training, and investing in military-to-military relationships. Let me share a few examples:

Operations: Our forces in the Middle East operate continuously on land, in the air, and on the sea; routinely conducting freedom of navigation operations, forward deployments, and port visits. They enhance stability and safeguard access to the global commons. U.S. military forces in the area are significant, with thousands of personnel deployed throughout the region, especially in and around the Arabian Gulf and in Afghanistan. Included in those numbers are U.S. soldiers and Marines with armor, artillery, and attack helicopters; highly trained Special Operations Forces; our most advanced aircraft; advanced surveillance assets; a wide array of missile defense capabilities, including Ballistic Missile Defense ships and PATRIOT batteries; and a large naval presence, including a carrier strike group, minesweeping capabilities, and an Afloat Forward Staging Base (AFSB).

Exercises: Military exercises increase proficiency and interoperability across all mission areas, including warfighting, counterterrorism, maritime security, and peacekeeping. USCENTCOM's extensive exercise program includes, on average, 35 significant exercises each quarter. In 2013, our training efforts included EXERCISE EAGLE RESOLVE, which was hosted by Qatar and included forces from 12 nations; EXERCISE EAGER LION in Jordan, which involved 8,000 personnel from 19 nations; and the International Mine Countermeasures Exercise in Bahrain, in which 40 nations and 35 ships participated. These are just a few of the hundreds of engagements conducted by all Services with foreign partners each year.

Senior Leader Engagement: In conjunction with the Department of State, our military maintains an aggressive schedule of leader interactions to strengthen relationships. These help us better understand regional perspectives on common security issues while fostering cooperation. For example, Chairman Dempsey participated in the Middle East Chiefs of Defense Conference in Jordan last August. Also, CENTCOM Commander, General Austin, and his service component commanders continuously engage their regional counterparts, such as at the regional Air Defense Chiefs' Conference in November, 2013. Engagements such as these allow us to listen to partner nation concerns, assure them of support, and demonstrate U.S. commitment to the region.

Building Partnership Capacity: We complement operations, exercises, and key leader engagement with efforts aimed at strengthening partner capacity. A key aspect of these initiatives are Foreign Military Sales and Foreign Military Financing programs, including more than $75 billion in U.S. arms sales to Gulf Cooperation Council states since 2007. We are also co-developing advanced Ballistic Missile Defense capabilities with Israel. International Military Education and Training is another key investment we are making to build enduring relationships with partner nation civilian and military leaders. We have trained over three thousand officers through this program over the last 13 years. Finally, we are working with partners throughout the region to help them better defend critical assets, both in the physical sense and in the cyber world, including military sites and key infrastructure.

Ladies and Gentlemen, your military's men and women are forward deployed every day in the Middle East in support of our national defense. We are proud of their efforts and their sacrifice.

Thank you for this opportunity to speak to your Committee this morning. And please accept my gratitude for all you have done for us.

United States Navy
Biography

Vice Admiral Frank Craig Pandolfe
DIRECTOR FOR STRATEGIC PLANS AND POLICY
JOINT STAFF, J-5

Vice Adm. Pandolfe is the Director for Strategic Plans and Policy (J-5), Joint Staff, the Pentagon, Washington, D.C. He provides strategic direction, policy guidance, and planning focus enabling the Chairman of the Joints Chiefs of Staff to provide best military advice to the President, the Secretary of Defense and the National Security Council. He assumed those duties Dec. 4, 2013.

He grew up in New England, graduated with distinction from the U.S. Naval Academy in 1980, and was awarded a doctorate in International Relations from the Fletcher School of Law and Diplomacy at Tufts University in 1987.

At-sea, he served in USS David R. Ray (DD 971), USS John Hancock (DD 981), USS Hue City (CG 66), and USS Forrestal (CV 59). He commanded USS Mitscher (DDG 57) from 1999 to 2001, earning three Battle Efficiency Awards for operational excellence and three Golden Anchor awards for superior retention. He subsequently commanded Destroyer Squadron 18 from 2003 to 2004, operating as sea combat commander for Enterprise Carrier Strike Group in support of Operation Iraqi Freedom. From 2008 to 2009, he led Theodore Roosevelt Carrier Strike Group on a combat deployment in support of Operation Enduring Freedom in Afghanistan.

Ashore, he was assigned to the Navy Staff as executive assistant to the Chief of Naval Operations, the Joint Staff as the Deputy Director for Joint Strategic Planning, and the White House Staff as military aide and advisor to the Vice President of the United States, and Director, Surface Warfare Division, OPNAV N86. Most recently, he served as the Commander, 6th Fleet and, Striking and Support Forces NATO.

Pandolfe's personal decorations include the Defense Superior Service Medal, Legion of Merit, Meritorious Service Medal, and additional individual, campaign, and unit awards.

Updated: 3 January 2014

WITNESS RESPONSES TO QUESTIONS ASKED DURING THE HEARING

FEBRUARY 11, 2014

RESPONSE TO QUESTION SUBMITTED BY MS. HANABUSA

Admiral PANDOLFE. Eagle Resolve Participating Countries: Bahrain, France, Iraq, Jordan, Kuwait, Lebanon, Oman, Qatar, Saudi Arabia, United Arab Emirates, United Kingdom, and the United States.

Eager Lion Participating Countries: Bahrain, Canada, Czech Republic, Egypt, France, Iraq, Italy, Jordan, Kuwait, Lebanon, Poland, Qatar, Saudi Arabia, Turkey, United Arab Emirates, United Kingdom, United States, and Yemen. [See page 23.]

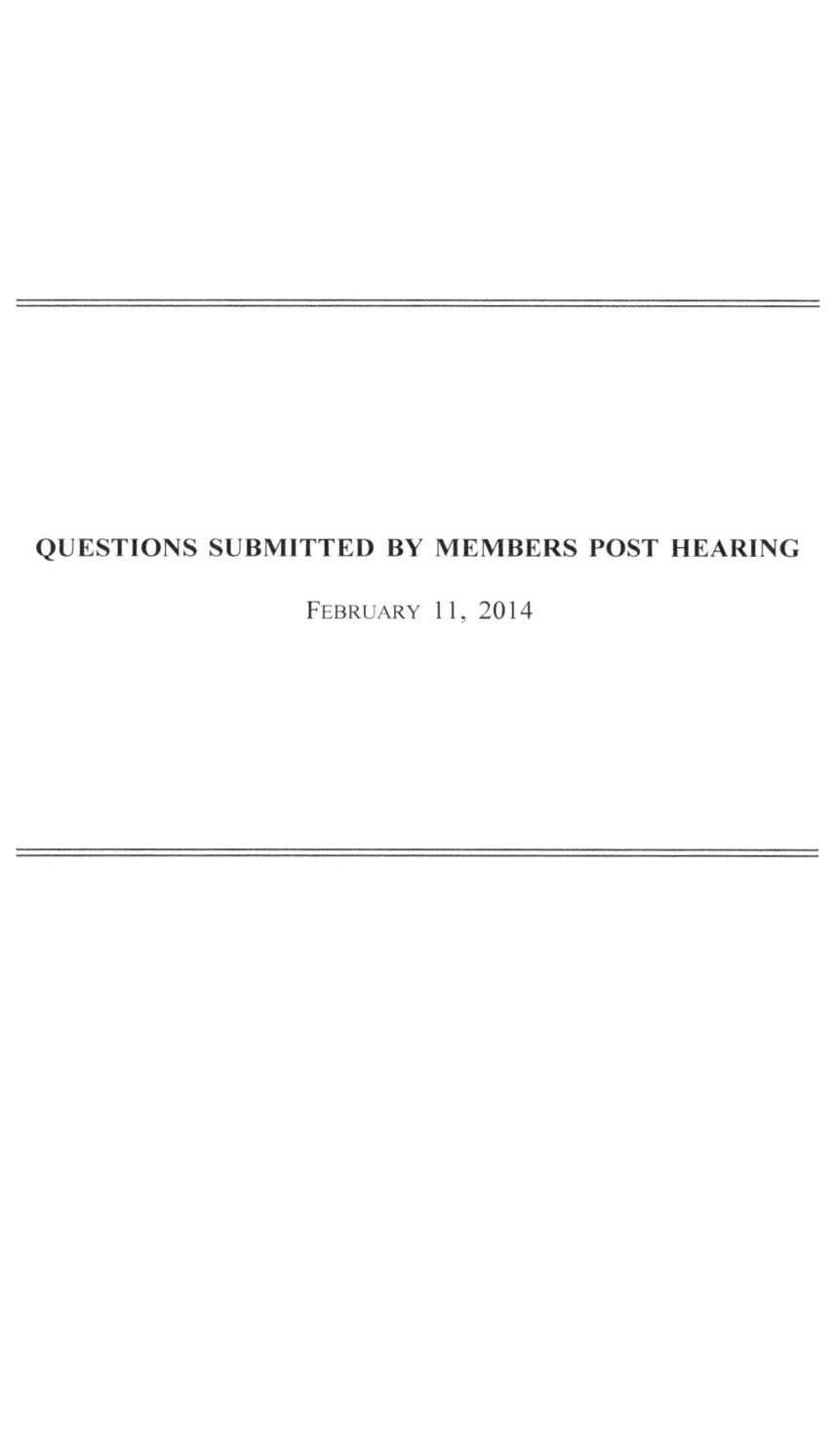

QUESTIONS SUBMITTED BY MEMBERS POST HEARING

FEBRUARY 11, 2014

QUESTIONS SUBMITTED BY MR. MCKEON

Mr. McKEON. Does it remain U.S. policy that all options, including military force, remain on the table to prevent Iran from developing a nuclear weapon?

Ambassador PATTERSON. This Administration views the prospect of a nuclear-armed Iran as unacceptable and is committed to preventing Iran from developing a nuclear weapon. The President has been consistent: the United States is committed to using all the necessary elements of American power to prevent Iran from acquiring a nuclear weapon. Although we continue to believe that there is time and space for a diplomatic solution to Iran's nuclear program, as the President has said, all options remain on the table.

Mr. McKEON. What are we doing to demonstrate to Iran that we are ready and willing to use force if necessary?

Ambassador PATTERSON. This Administration has made non-proliferation one of its top priorities. We view the prospect of a nuclear-armed Iran as unacceptable and are committed to preventing Iran from acquiring a nuclear weapon. We have implemented the strongest, most comprehensive sanctions regime to date against the Iranian government.

The United States is committed to using all the necessary elements of American power to prevent Iran from acquiring a nuclear weapon. Although we continue to believe that there is time and space for a diplomatic solution, as the President has said, all options remain on the table.

Mr. McKEON. Iran is in a position where it could break out and produce enough highly enriched uranium for a weapon in less than two months. Is the U.S. military prepared to act in such a narrow timeframe to respond to an Iranian breakout attempt?

Ambassador PATTERSON. I am not going to speculate about military action or discuss military planning. President Obama has pledged repeatedly that all options remain on the table.

Mr. McKEON. What impact did the lack of U.S. military action in Syria have on Iran's view of the credibility of the U.S. threat of force to stop its nuclear quest?

Ambassador PATTERSON. When the President stated his willingness to order a limited strike against the Asad regime in response to the brazen use of chemical weapons, he did not do so lightly. The purpose of such a strike, as the President said, would have been to deter and degrade the regime's ability to use chemical weapons.

The threat of force in Syria remains credible because it is in the security interest of the United States and the world to meaningfully enforce the international prohibition against use of chemical weapons. The President has made it clear that all options remain on the table. However, as the President said, he preferred a diplomatic resolution to this issue and we are implementing the agreement reached in Geneva in September. This diplomatic resolution will meet our objectives by ensuring that the regime can never again deploy these terrible weapons.

Likewise, the Administration seeks a diplomatic resolution to the concerns of Iran's nuclear program. The Administration is committed to the nonproliferation of weapons of mass destruction and views the prospect of a nuclear-armed Iran as unacceptable and remains committed to preventing Iran from developing a nuclear weapon.

The United States is committed to using all the necessary elements of American power to prevent Iran from developing a nuclear weapon. Although we continue to believe that there is time and space for a diplomatic solution to Iran's nuclear program, as the President has said, all options remain on the table.

Mr. McKEON. What steps are the United States taking to mitigate the impact of unfolding Middle East events on Israel's QME?

Ambassador PATTERSON. The United States is committed to helping Israel maintain its QME, defined as Israel's ability to counter and defeat credible military threats from any individual state, coalition of states or non-state actors, while sustaining minimal damage or casualties. This policy was written into law in 2008, but it has long been a fundamental tenet of U.S. policy and a cornerstone of the U.S.-Israel security relationship.

The Administration is regularly assessing the capabilities of the region's militaries and non-state actors to ensure Israel maintains its qualitative military edge (QME). We are also taking full advantage of the consultative and political mechanisms currently in place to respond to and act on Israel's concerns.

In addition to fulfilling the requirements of the Naval Vessel Transfer Act of 2008, the United States protects Israel's QME in a number of important ways. 1) Israel is the leading recipient of Foreign Military Financing (FMF). In FY 2013, which marked the fifth year of a 10-year, $30 billion MOU, Israel received $2.94 billion in FMF, slightly less than the $3.1 billion request level due to sequestration. We requested the full $3.1 billion in FY 2014; 2) Israel is the only country authorized to use one-quarter of its FMF funding for domestic defense procurement, which provides significant flexibility in meeting immediate procurement needs and supporting the Israeli defense industry; 3) Israel has privileged access to advanced U.S. military equipment, such as the F–35 Joint Strike Fighter and, more recently, the MV–22 Osprey; 4) the United States is cooperating with Israel, using DOD appropriated funding, to develop a comprehensive air and missile defense system that protects Israel against ballistic and cruise missile threats; and 5) the United States has provided additional funding outside of State's annual FMF request to support the expansion and acceleration of the Israeli-developed Iron Dome short-range rocket defense system. In FY 2011, Congress provided an additional $205 million for the procurement of additional Iron Dome systems. We provided an additional $70 million in FY2012 for Iron Dome systems and another $195 million in FY 2013 and $220M in FY 2014. The Administration has requested $175.9M for FY 2015.

Mr. McKEON. How is the United States ensuring that arms sales to the region do not undermine Israel's QME?

Ambassador PATTERSON. The Administration has sought to enhance security cooperation with and between U.S. partners in the Middle East. The United States is engaged in extensive efforts to ensure its partners have credible military capabilities to respond to potential regional threats. An essential part of this approach is providing our partners access, when appropriate, to military technologies critical to their national defense. These sales will also allow U.S. security partners to bear a greater share of the burden for regional security.

Enhancing the capabilities of our Arab partners does not come at the expense of Israel's security. This administration is committed to strengthening security cooperation with Israel and safeguarding its qualitative military edge (QME). We do not proceed with the release of U.S. defense articles or services that could pose a risk to our allies and partners or compromise regional security in the Middle East.

Israel remains, by a significant margin, the leading recipient of foreign military financing and the Israel Defense Forces enjoy privileged access to the most advanced U.S. military equipment, such as the F–35 Joint Strike Fighter and the V–22 Osprey.

Mr. McKEON. Do you share Director Clapper's concern about the threat foreign fighters in Syria pose to the United States or our allies like Israel? How are we addressing this potential threat?

Ambassador PATTERSON. The U.S. government is extremely concerned by the threat posed by foreign fighter travel to Syria and potential implications for broader regional stability as a result. Furthermore, we are worried about the potential for these fighters, some of whom have connections with al-Qa'ida elements, to plan for and conduct attacks outside Syria, particularly against U.S. and other Western interests.

We have been in close consultation with our partners in Europe and the Middle East on this matter. Effective coordination and collaboration with these partners is crucial in mitigating foreign fighter flows. Our discussions with partners are focusing on enhancing information sharing, border security measures to deny departure or entry of known or suspected extremist travelers, effective watchlisting, law enforcement cooperation, and measures to counter violent extremist messages and recruitment. We plan to intensify this engagement over the coming months.

Mr. McKEON. What is the United States doing to stop the flow of foreign fighters to Syria?

Ambassador PATTERSON. We have been in close consultation on this matter with our partners in Europe and the Middle East, particularly over the past year. Effective coordination and collaboration with these partners is crucial in mitigating foreign fighter flows. To that end, the State Department has been leading U.S. interagency outreach with key partners in Europe and the Middle East. Our discussions are focusing on enhancing information sharing, border security, and law enforcement cooperation, in addition to efforts to counter violent extremist messages and recruitment.

Mr. McKEON. What challenges do you foresee in Lebanon given the increasing incidents of violence across the country? How can the United States minimize the threat of violence aimed at Israel from its northern border?

Ambassador PATTERSON. U.S. policy in Lebanon is focused on bolstering Lebanon's stability and sovereignty and countering extremist influences, both foreign and domestic. Lebanon has faced a rising tempo of terrorist attacks in the last six months that have killed and wounded hundreds of civilians across the country. These attacks are directly related to the spillover of the Syria crisis into Lebanon.

Another challenge is that Lebanon currently hosts almost a million refugees from Syria, and more enter Lebanon every day. These refugees, who live in communities across the country, strain the basic infrastructure of the nation as well as tax local municipalities' abilities to scale up services to meet rising needs.

Increasing sectarian violence and a steady influx of refugees from Syria threatens Lebanon's stability. It is imperative that we continue our assistance to and partnership with the Lebanese Armed Forces (LAF) and Internal Security Forces (ISF); our long-standing, community-based USAID programming; our strong support for moderate leaders, such as President Michel Sleiman; our continuous engagement with mainstream political actors, including March 14 leaders; and our whole-of-government approach to countering Hizballah activity around the world.

Our security assistance to the LAF and ISF is intended to develop functioning, non-sectarian state institutions that gain respect from all Lebanese citizens in order to show the Lebanese people that they do not need militias for protection or to advance their political aims. Sustained U.S. support, particularly in the face of increasing domestic and regional tensions, has maintained and improved the LAF's capabilities as a national security force. A stronger LAF would contribute to stability on Lebanon's border with Israel, help mitigate the spillover effects of the violence in Syria, and serve as an increasingly effective counterweight to Hizballah.

Working closely with the United Nations Interim Force in Lebanon (UNIFIL), the LAF's performance in southern Lebanon has added to stability along the Blue Line with Israel. UN Security Council Resolution 1701 calls upon Lebanon to disarm Lebanon's militias—a goal we support through our training and equipping of the LAF and the ISF as the sole legitimate defense forces in Lebanon. Part of UNIFIL's mission is to keep the Blue Line secure, and it also trains with the LAF to increase its capability to monitor the border and provide security. The LAF is not yet fully able to provide security throughout the entire area under UNIFIL's mandate, but with our assistance, further UNIFIL training, and other international support, the LAF's capabilities are improving.

Mr. McKEON. Does it remain U.S. policy that all options, including military force, remain on the table to prevent Iran from developing a nuclear weapon?

Ms. SLOTKIN. Yes. Although diplomacy remains the preferred means to resolve international concerns regarding Iran's nuclear program, all options—including military option—remain on the table to prevent Iran from developing a nuclear weapon.

Mr. McKEON. What are we doing to demonstrate to Iran that we are ready and willing to use force if necessary?

Ms. SLOTKIN. Iran is well aware of our force presence and the significant capabilities of the U.S. military in the region. We have about 35,000 forces deployed in and immediately around the Gulf region. We have over 40 ships in the broader Middle East region, to include a carrier strike group. We also have deployed an array of missile defense capabilities, advanced intelligence, surveillance and reconnaissance assets, as well as some of our most sophisticated aircraft. Our assets conducted approximately 50 transits through the Strait of Hormuz just during the last six months of 2013. Finally, our forces and personnel conducted and participated in over 50 multilateral and bilateral training exercises in the broader Middle East region last year. All of these serve as a constant reminder that the United States is ready and willing to use force to advance its core interests.

Mr. McKEON. Iran is in a position where it could break out and produce enough highly enriched uranium for a weapon in less than two months. Is the U.S. military prepared to act in such a narrow timeframe to respond to an Iranian breakout attempt?

Ms. SLOTKIN. Given this is an open forum, let me say simply that I am confident the U.S. military is ready and able to respond quickly and decisively to a variety of contingencies around the world, including one involving Iran, if necessary.

Mr. McKEON. What impact did the lack of U.S. military action in Syria have on Iran's view of the credibility of the U.S. threat of force to stop its nuclear quest?

Ms. SLOTKIN. The Intelligence Community is best positioned to answer this question. However, it was the credible threat of military force that helped bring about the diplomatic resolution on chemical weapons elimination in Syria. Our preference is to resolve issues through diplomacy, but the United States is prepared to execute military action should it become necessary.

Mr. McKEON. What steps are the United States taking to mitigate the impact of unfolding Middle East events on Israel's QME?

Ms. SLOTKIN. As Secretary Hagel has said, "Our commitment to Israel's security is ironclad and unyielding." In the midst of the uncertainty and instability that has plagued the Middle East in recent years, the Department of Defense has worked diligently to ensure that Israel's qualitative military edge is maintained. In addition to providing $3.1 billion in Foreign Military Financing (FMF) each year—the most FMF provided to any country in history—the United States has made sure that Israel has access to the most advanced military capabilities possible, including the F–35 and the V–22 Osprey. Access to these types of advanced capabilities, combined with an unprecedented level of FMF to purchase them, will ensure that Israel's qualitative military edge is maintained for the next generation.

Mr. MCKEON. How is the United States ensuring that arms sales to the region do not undermine Israel's QME?

Ms. SLOTKIN. The cornerstone of the U.S. security assurance to Israel is the United States' support to Israel's qualitative military edge (QME). Israel must have the ability to defeat any adversary—anytime, anywhere. As you know, the importance of ensuring Israel's QME is not just based on shared values and interests, but is also based on U.S. law. This law provides that any proposed sale or export of defense articles or services to the Middle East will include a determination that the sale or export will not adversely affect Israel's QME. Working with the Department of State, the Department of Defense will continue to ensure that, in accordance with this law, arms sales to the Middle East will not undermine Israel's QME.

Mr. MCKEON. Do you share Director Clapper's concern about the threat foreign fighters in Syria pose to the United States or our allies like Israel? How are we addressing this potential threat?

Ms. SLOTKIN. I agree this issue is of concern, both to the United States and our partners in the region, including Israel. We are monitoring this issue closely and working with partners in the Middle East to address this threat. We are providing assistance to Lebanon and Jordan to strengthen their ability to secure their borders, including, for example, by providing equipment and training to supplement the Jordan Border Security Program. We are also working with Turkey and Iraq to determine how to stem the flow of foreign fighters into the region.

In addition, DOD will continue to support the efforts of other U.S. departments and agencies to strengthen elements of the moderate Syrian opposition so they can better degrade terrorists' ability to attack the homeland and U.S. interests abroad.

Mr. MCKEON. What is the United States doing to stop the flow of foreign fighters to Syria?

Ms. SLOTKIN. We are working with our partners in the region and our European allies, many of whom share our concerns on this issue, to develop the most effective options to stem the flow of fighters into and out of Syria.

To that end, we are supporting Syria's neighbors in enhancing their border security, and have provided assistance to both Lebanon and Jordan; we are working with Turkey and Iraq to determine how we can more effectively help those nations deal with foreign fighters crossing their borders. We are also closely coordinating with Israel to make sure Israel can defend itself against violent extremist threats in Syria.

The Department is working with our interagency and international partners to organize our efforts to monitor the activities and movements of extremists in the region, and enable U.S. and international efforts to disrupt foreign fighter flows and potential extremist attacks. The whole of the U.S. government is coordinating closely on measures we can take to support this top priority as well as Ambassador Brafke, who was recently named as State's Senior Advisor for Partner Engagement on Syria Foreign Fighters.

Mr. MCKEON. What challenges do you foresee in Lebanon given the increasing incidents of violence across the country? How can the United States minimize the threat of violence aimed at Israel from its northern border?

Ms. SLOTKIN. Unfortunately, as long as the violence in Syria continues, we expect that Lebanon will continue to suffer from spillover violence and humanitarian-related pressures. Terrorist attacks in Lebanon are on the rise. The Lebanese Armed Forces (LAF) have taken a variety of measures to maintain stability in Lebanon and to counter the destabilizing effects of the Syrian conflict on Lebanon's security. The Lebanese Armed Forces' willingness to exercise its role in Lebanon has made it a target as well.

Our continued engagement with and assistance to the LAF are extremely important at this time of increased challenges to Lebanon's stability. We remain concerned with Iran's destabilizing activities in Lebanon and its partnership with Hizballah. We view the Lebanese Armed Forces' emergence as the sole legitimate defense force as a critical component of Lebanon's long-term stability and development. The Lebanese Armed Forces has proved to be a reliable partner in Lebanon, and continuing to make it a stronger, more effective institution will help to ensure that Lebanon remains stable and capable of protecting its borders, thereby reducing the risk of attacks on Israel from terrorist elements that may seek to use Lebanon as a launching pad for violence.

Mr. McKEON. Iran is in a position where it could break out and produce enough highly enriched uranium for a weapon in less than two months. Is the U.S. military prepared to act in such a narrow timeframe to respond to an Iranian breakout attempt?

Admiral PANDOLFE. DNI assesses that Iran will need up to one year or longer to produce a testable nuclear weapon from the point of decision to do so. Thus, as discussed in the hearing, we continue to maintain a strong military posture in the Gulf region.

Mr. McKEON. What impact did the lack of U.S. military action in Syria have on Iran's view of the credibility of the U.S. threat of force to stop its nuclear quest?

Admiral PANDOLFE. The Director of National Intelligence (DNI) has assessed that Iran is trying to balance the conflicting objectives of improving its nuclear capabilities with avoiding severe repercussions, such as a military strike or sanctions. The DNI does not know if Iran will eventually decide to build nuclear weapons.

Mr. McKEON. What steps are the United States taking to mitigate the impact of unfolding Middle East events on Israel's QME [qualitative military edge]?

Admiral PANDOLFE. DOD is able to mitigate the impact of unfolding Middle East events on Israel's QME through the sale of advanced technology to Israel, participation in combined training and exercises, and support for active missile defense efforts in Israel.

Annual Foreign Military Financing (FMF) grants of $3.1 billion support Israel's QME. FMF, along with national funds and U.S. missile defense appropriations to Israel, represent over $18 billion in Foreign Military Sales and Direct Commercial Contract purchases. To maintain QME, the U.S. delivered the C–130J to replace Israel's aging C–130E fleet and has agreed to provide advanced systems such as the F–35 and V–22 along with attack helicopters, Patriot Air Defense Systems, and advanced fighter aircraft radar systems. In addition, Israel benefits from the $1.4 billion War Reserve Stock Allies-Israel program that includes Patriot missiles, bombs, and other weapons in country for use in a contingency.

Many exercises offer DOD the opportunity to work with Israeli counterparts. These include Juniper Cobra, Austere Challenge, Reliant Mermaid, Noble Dina, Noble Shirley, Blue Flag and other BMD and command and control exercises. These exercises address emerging challenges and increase our combined capabilities, interoperability, and readiness.

DOD also supports Israel's multi-layered missile and rocket defense. By the end of FY 2014, the United States will have provided over $700 million for production of Iron Dome batteries in addition to the $3.1 billion Israel receives in FMF. In FY 2015, DOD plans to provide an additional $176 million for Iron Dome.

Mr. McKEON. Do you share Director Clapper's concern about the threat foreign fighters in Syria pose to the United States or our allies like Israel? How are we addressing this potential threat?

Admiral PANDOLFE. I share Director Clapper's concern over the foreign fighter threat in Syria. Some foreign fighters are joining units with known links to terrorist organizations. DOD continues to pursue a strategy of capacity-building, security assistance, and intelligence-sharing with our international partners to aid in combating violent extremist threats emanating from Syria.

Mr. McKEON. What is the United States doing to stop the flow of foreign fighters to Syria?

Admiral PANDOLFE. The DOD pursues a strategy of capacity building, security assistance, and intelligence sharing with international partners to disrupt the flow of foreign fighters to Syria. Example capacity building programs include the Jordan Border Security Project to improve ground surveillance and communication and utilization of Section 1206 Global Train and Equip funding to improve Lebanon border security.

Security assistance comes in the form of Foreign Military Financing to Iraq, Jordan, and Lebanon that totaled $826 million in FY 2013. In January, DOD expedited a $203 million Government of Iraq request to purchase arms and ammunition to facilitate response to extremist attacks throughout the country.

Expanded intelligence sharing with Jordan, Iraq, and Turkey also aids DOD's strategy to address the foreign fighter flow to Syria. This approach involves coordination across the interagency.

www.ingramcontent.com/pod-product-compliance
Lightning Source LLC
Chambersburg PA
CBHW081328310526
45789CB00018B/2586